T0207565

# THE NON-JEWISH JEW
and other essays

# THE NON-JEWISH JEW

## and other essays

ISAAC DEUTSCHER

Edited with an Introduction by
Tamara Deutscher

VERSO

London • New York

Acknowledgement is due to the following for permission to reprint certain essays: *The Economist*, *The Observer*, *The Jewish Quarterly*, *The New Left Review*, *The Reporter Magazine* and the World Jewish Congress.

This edition published by Verso 2017
First published by Oxford University Press 1968
© Isaac Deutscher 1968, 2017
Introduction © Tamara Deutscher 1968, 2017

3 5 7 9 10 8 6 4 2

**Verso**
UK: 6 Meard Street, London W1F 0EG
US: 388 Atlantic Ave, Brooklyn, NY 11217
versobooks.com

Verso is the imprint of New Left Books

ISBN-13: 978-1-78663-082-7
ISBN-13: 978-1-78663-083-4 (UK EBK)
ISBN-13: 978-1-78663-084-1 (US EBK)

**British Library Cataloguing in Publication Data**
A catalogue record for this book is available from the British Library

**Library of Congress Cataloging-in-Publication Data**
A catalog record for this book is available from the Library of Congress

Printed in the USA

# CONTENTS

# EDITOR'S NOTE

THIS volume of essays is published posthumously. Isaac Deutscher, had he lived, would have revised his own work more thoroughly. I have decided to interfere as little as possible with those essays which at one time or another had already appeared in print: here and there a footnote has been added or an excision made. I have taken the responsibility for editing the text of the lecture on 'The Russian Revolution and the Jewish Problem' which was left uncompleted; the essay 'Who is a Jew?' required a more thorough work of selection and compression.

In a collection of lectures, articles, and interviews devoted to one particular subject, though it may be approached from different angles, some overlapping is unavoidable. The reader will be left in no doubt, however, that Isaac Deutscher, in his views on the most complex role and tragic fate of Jews in Europe and in their own national state, remained consistent throughout.

I can only trust that in my work on these essays I have succeeded in preserving faithfully, and in all instances, Isaac Deutscher's thought.

I am grateful to Dr. R. Miliband and Mr. D. Singer for reading the volume before it was sent off to the Publisher; to Mr. John Bell and Mr. Dan M. Davin, of Oxford University Press, for assistance and valuable advice; and I would also like to thank my friends and neighbours Mr. and Mrs. E. F. C. Ludowyk for their affection and constant encouragement.

*London, January* 1968                                    T.D.

# ISAAC DEUTSCHER

## 1907–1967

Isaac Deutscher's reputation was made first of all as a poet when at the age of sixteen his first poems were published in Polish literary periodicals. His early verse, still remembered by the scattered remnants of his reading public, has strong echoes of Jewish mysticism, *motifs* of Jewish history and mythology, and fuses Polish romanticism with Jewish lyrical folklore in an attempt to bridge the gulf between Polish and Yiddish culture. He also translated a great deal of Hebrew, Latin, German, and Yiddish poetry into Polish.

As an extramural student he attended lectures on literature, history, and philosophy at the medieval Yagellon University in Cracow. Evenings devoted to readings of his poems became notable events in the life of this artistic and scholarly Polish city.

At the age of eighteen he left Cracow for Warsaw; he also left poetry for literary criticism, and a more profound study of philosophy, of economics, and of Marxism. About 1927 he joined the outlawed Polish Communist Party and very soon became the chief editor of the clandestine and semi-clandestine communist press. In 1931 he travelled widely in the U.S.S.R., acquainting himself with the economic conditions of the country under its first Five Year Plan. He declined offers of academic positions at the Universities of Moscow and Minsk as a professor of history of socialism and Marxist theory. In the following year he was expelled from the Communist Party.

The official reason for his expulsion was that he 'exaggerated the danger of Nazism and was spreading panic in the communist ranks'. Soon after his return from the U.S.S.R. he had founded, together with three or four comrades, the first anti-Stalinist opposition in the Polish Communist Party. His group protested against the party line according to which Social Democracy and Nazism were 'not antipodes but twins'; and when one day the communist underground papers came out with the headline 'Danger of Barbarism Over Europe', the chief editor was expelled from the party and excommunicated. From that day two sleuths shadowed him: one employed by the Polish police, and the other a volunteer from the Stalinist party cell.

In April 1939 Isaac Deutscher left Warsaw for London as a correspondent of a Polish-Jewish paper which had employed him for fourteen years as a proof reader. It was his good fortune that, when the war broke out and he was cut off from his income, a Yiddish newspaper in London rejected his contribution. This compelled him to apply himself with the utmost energy and zeal to learning English. Flanked by dictionaries, grammars, and textbooks, he wrote his first article in English and sent it off to *The Economist*. It was published the following week and from that time his contributions appeared regularly.

In 1940 Isaac Deutscher joined the Polish Army in Scotland, but most of his 'army life' was spent in the punitive camps as a 'dangerous and subversive element'—the return for his unceasing protests against the anti-semitism rampant in that army. Released in 1942, he joined the staff of *The Economist* and became its expert on Soviet affairs, military commentator, and chief European correspondent. He also joined the staff of *The Observer* for which he became, *inter alia*, a roving European correspondent writing under the pen-name Peregrine.

In 1946–7 he left Fleet Street and regular journalism for less ephemeral work. *Stalin, A Political Biography* was published in 1949. Described as 'the most controversial biography of our time', it went into very many editions and appeared in a dozen languages. The enlarged 1967 edition contains a postscript on Stalin's last years.

The publication of *Stalin* led to the recognition of Isaac Deutscher as an authority on Soviet affairs and the historian of the Russian revolution; his *Trotsky* trilogy—*The Prophet Armed* (1954), *The Prophet Unarmed* (1959) and *The Prophet Outcast* (1963)—established his reputation also as a master of English prose. His biography of Trotsky is based on detailed research into the Trotsky Archives at Harvard University. Much of the material contained in the third volume is unique, for he received special permission from Trotsky's widow, the late Natalya Sedov, to read through the Closed Section of the Archives which, by the will of Trotsky himself, is to remain unopened till the end of the century.

Isaac Deutscher planned to conclude his biographical series with a study of Lenin, and he often expressed the hope that his works would be seen as 'a single essay in a Marxist analysis of the revolution of our age and also as a triptych of some artistic unity'.

As G. M. Trevelyan Lecturer at Cambridge University for 1966–7, Deutscher addressed overflow audiences and was rewarded by their extraordinary attentiveness and warm-hearted response. The same response was granted him during his six weeks' stay at the State University of New York at Binghamton, Harpur College, and also when he lectured at New York University, Princeton, Harvard, and Columbia in the spring of 1967. The G. M. Trevelyan Lectures, under the title *The Unfinished Revolution,* appeared almost simultaneously in fourteen or fifteen countries. But none of his books, though they went into many editions and were translated into many languages, has so far been published in the countries of the Soviet bloc. There is evidence, however, that even there he has not a few courageous and devoted readers.

A speaker of spellbinding powers and a debater of great argumentative force, Isaac Deutscher frequently addressed large audiences on both sides of the Atlantic. In 1965 he took part in the first Teach-In on Vietnam, in the course of which fifteen thousand students gathered on the Berkeley University campus to listen to his indictment of the Cold War.

Such was Isaac Deutscher's extraordinary vitality that, although engaged almost single-handed on his monumental literary work, he still followed the course of current politics with passionate interest, and for fourteen years his analyses of major international events were widely read in the main newspapers in Europe, in the U.S.A., Canada, Japan, India, and Latin America.

He worked till the very last day of his life and died in Rome on 19 August 1967.

T.D.

*May* 1968

# The Education of a Jewish Child

DURING the last few years of his life Isaac Deutscher intended to write his autobiography, or rather that part of it which would tell of his childhood and youth. He wanted to show the readers of the mature author what his origin was, and the background he came from. The world he came from does not exist any more—the world so brutally wrecked, tortured, massacred, and obliterated. It will never be recreated. It can live only in the memory and sensitivity of those who survived. Did Isaac want to save this world from oblivion, to paint for the younger generation of today the panorama of Jewish religious and secular life, as he knew it, before the fiery deluge of Nazism fell on it?

He viewed with scepticism the numerous attempts of Jewish organizations in the West to tell the story: to collect documents, factual accounts, diaries, and all sorts of material in order to keep alive the traditions and the history of pre-war European Jewry. This artificial respiration, as he saw it, would not bring back the breath and the pulse of life into the dead body. No wealth of documentary evidence, however faithful, could convey the mood, the atmosphere, the spiritual and intellectual climate of this closely knit community which has been destroyed and in which Isaac spent the most impressionable years of his life.

Were they really his most impressionable years?

It seemed to me that it was not the historian's rational urge to look into the past in order to make it comprehensible to others or to show how it might lead to the present that prompted Isaac to write about his childhood. He liked to go back in his thoughts and reminiscences to his earliest days precisely because they were to him so unbelievably far away that they appeared unreal. A great gulf separated him, the Khassidic child prodigy of Chrzanów,[1] immersed in the Talmud and the Torah, or studying at the Court of the Wonderrabbi—the Tsadik of Gere—from the atheist, the Marxist revolutionary, addressing in his sonorous, rich, and fluent English tens of thousands of American students on the shores of the Pacific Ocean. That gulf was so immense that it baffled and fascinated him.

It was just this fascination that one could detect in Isaac's manner of recalling his early, very early days. It both amazed and amused him that the memories he was recalling, the incidents he was relating, were really about himself. For us, no less than for him, it was not easy to see him as a little boy, with a thick black crop of hair, curled sidelocks, making his way, a flickering oil lamp in his hand, at five o'clock in the morning, through the snow and mud of sleepy Chrzanów, with the privilege, as the best pupil, of waking up the *Rebe*.

'I would knock on the door, first timidly, then harder and harder, until a glimmer of candle light showed in the window. *The Rebbetzin* would let me in, muttering something through her shawl. I was left standing by the door until the *Rebe* appeared: thin, gaunt, with his muddy beard

[1] Chrzanów is about 20 miles west of Cracow, 10 miles north of Oświęcim (Auschwitz). In 1907, the year of Isaac's birth, Chrzanów had 6,000 inhabitants, of which 4,500 were Jews.

all dishevelled. We went to the Synagogue for morning prayers. He was holding my hand, but I was small, very small, and he was tall and walked fast, and I seemed to be dangling from his long arm, barely touching the ground.' Was this child really myself? was the unuttered question behind this tale. Did Isaac's childhood really lead him to his manhood?

Originally, his ancestors came, in the sixteenth century, to Galicia from Nuremberg. They bore the name of Ashkenazy ('German' in Hebrew). There were so many printers among them that competition in business led to confusion and constant quarrels. One branch of the clan then changed the name to Deutscher. Even among the Deutschers several printing shops competed with one another.

Isaac was named after his great-grandfather—a learned Talmudic scholar, a man of frightful temper and fanatic convictions. He viewed Khassidism as a deviation from orthodoxy. It was a sect in which plebeian elements were in revolt against the pomposity and strictness of the Jewish religious Establishment. One of the sons of the old Reb Isaac was attracted to Khassidism with its more joyous view of life and its more lax discipline, and he swore allegiance to the Tsadik of Gere. This was an unusual occurrence among the Galician Jews.

The Gere Rabbi had his Court on the other side of the frontier, in so-called Congress Poland, and restrictions on travel, especially for Jews, made pilgrimages nearly impossible. Reb Isaac's wrath, when he learned that his son was on the way to Gere, was terrible. He behaved in an unheard-of manner: he had recourse to secular and non-Jewish authorities; he even enlisted the help of the Austrian police. He denounced his disobedient son, telegraphed the frontier guards, and requested that the 'smuggler' be brought back under escort. He succeeded, but only for a time. The prodigal son was more fortunate in his next escapade. Till the end of his days he remained a staunch adherent of Khassidism, stayed with the Gere Tsadik and died peacefully of old age in his *Beth Midrash*—House of Prayers—on the very holy evening of the New Year. He was buried with great honours near the tomb of the founder of the Gere dynasty. Despite the wrath of Reb Isaac, Khassidism conquered the Deutscher family.

Jacob Kopel, Isaac's father, a man of great learning and culture, had his period of restlessness and defiance too. In his youth he travelled in Germany and devoted himself to the study of the archives of the Jewish communities in the Rhineland. For years he was engaged in writing an exhaustive history of the Jews based on very thorough, original, and painstaking research. When the manuscript was ready, he went back home. Here he met the hostility not so much of his father but of his mother. The fanatical God-fearing woman suspected some heretical inclinations in her son's pursuits. Her duty, as she conceived it, was to save him in time. She threw the formidable manuscript into the fire.

Jacob Kopel seemed to be crushed by this blow. He submitted, he conformed, he forgave his mother, but the experience marked him for life. He remained torn between the sense of duty, of allegiance to the strict orthodoxy of his forefathers and an insatiable intellectual curiosity which bred doubts and tempted him not perhaps to abandon Judaism, but certainly to go beyond and outside it. He did not rebel. Like his father and grandfather, he became a printer and he gave all his loving care and attention to other people's manuscripts.

Under the imprint *Buchrückerei Deutscher* appeared religious works, philosophical dissertations, historical treatises and even textbooks of mathematics and algebra, in Hebrew, German, and Latin. It was a matter of great pride that the famous edition of the Bible with Gustave Doré's illustrations came from the Deutschers' printing presses. This slight deviation from orthodoxy was glossed over in this case; professional satisfaction weighed more than strict adherence to the Mosaic law which frowns on any 'graven images'.

Isaac, his son, was the oldest of the three children born to Jacob Kopel Deutscher of his second marriage. He was, according to the family tradition, destined to be a rabbi; and his father saw him not as an ordinary rabbi ministering to the needs of the faithful, but as a great Talmudic scholar. On his firstborn son the father focussed all his frustrated and thwarted intellectual ambition. He had good reasons.

As a child Isaac was at one with his Khassidic uncles, friends, neighbours. Their archaic religion, their prejudices, beliefs and fears, their anachronistic mode of life was his. A precocious boy, with a fantastic memory, capacious mind and an uncommon ability for abstract thinking, Isaac became a rabbi at the tender age of thirteen. The orthodox Jewish community of Leghorn had already been making inquiries about the future plans for this child prodigy, hinting at a resplendent career among the rich and dignified Italian Jews.

But by the time the thirteen year old was celebrating his *Bar Mitzva* and delivering the learned discourse on the strength of which he was 'consecrated' as a rabbi, he had already begun to question (as he was always going to) some of the assumptions of what he was supposed to believe in—then the assumptions of his religion. No wonder: the

N.J.J.—2

subject of his dissertation could not have been more scholastic and archaic or more remote from the pulse of life.

'Nearly a hundred rabbis descended on our little town to listen to my discourse, to judge it, and either to give me their blessing or to withhold it', Isaac related. For his father, for the whole family, indeed for the whole community, this was the supreme test. Isaac was tense but not overawed. He remembered his father's advice: Stand straight, collect your thoughts, and when you know what you want to say, speak clearly and loudly. It was one of those parental injunctions repeated over and over again with which all children always get impatient but always remember.

Dressed in a new *kapota* of pure silk made especially for the occasion, little Iciu—as he was affectionately called—'stood straight, collected his thoughts' and started on a two hour discourse on the theme of Kikiyon:

Once in seventy years a bird appears over the world. The bird is big and beautiful and unlike all other birds. Its name is Kikiyon. This curious name, probably Greek in origin, has never been explained. When the bird makes its flight—once in seventy years—it spits on the earth, and it spits only once. This saliva is extremely precious; it has miraculous qualities, for it can cure any illness or deformity. What Isaac had to debate and give his most considered opinion on was this: Is the bird's saliva *kosher* or *treyfe?* In other words, does it fulfil the requirements of the Jewish ritual with regard to food or not? Isaac quoted at length all that had been written on the subject before—all the commentaries, all the learned discussions that had been going on for millennia among the wisest of the wise. He showed command of his sources and a capacity to deal with the most abstruse details. His audience sat enthralled and in complete silence.

They nodded their heads admiringly. Then, after a short consultation, they pronounced him, inevitably, fit and worthy to become a rabbi.

'When I finished speaking, congratulations were showered on me. My mother, all my aunts and uncles, embraced and kissed me, crying and laughing at the same time. My father tried to conceal his deep satisfaction and pride. I felt relieved. But an unexpected sense of embarrassment, of unease, suddenly overtook me. I was putting on an act and I was pleased with the theatrical side of my performance.'

Was this exercise in scholastic debate of any use? Was it perhaps a lesson in abstract thinking, a training in mental speculation? Was it Montaigne's 'gymnastics of the mind'? Was it perhaps an early practice in successful polemical disputation? To those questions Isaac's reply was always a very categorical 'No'. On the contrary. 'All this pseudo-knowledge cluttered and strained my memory, took me away from real life, from real learning, from real knowledge of the world around me. It stunted my physical and mental development.'

Into the preparation of the Kikiyon treatise did indeed go long hours of study and reading. At the age of four Isaac had been sent to the *kheder*, the Jewish religious school, of which he always spoke with disgust. It was a dirty and fetid hole with twenty or thirty boys squeezed tightly together on wooden benches, with the unwashed and unkempt teacher drilling into his charges the *alef, beis, gyml*, the Hebrew alphabet, the Bible and the Scriptures in a mechanical monotonous singsong. Very often the teacher had recourse to the stick with which he could reach the head, the face, or the shoulders of an unruly pupil.

There was another form of punishment too: 'On my very

first day at the *kheder* I was terrified by the "basin punish-ment",' Isaac used to recall. A bad student would be told to strip naked and had to stand in front of the class with his feet in a chipped enamel bowl. 'I vowed firmly that this would never, never happen to me. I strained every nerve to follow the words of the teacher and to be always ready to answer any question.' Only once was poor Iciu smacked across the face. His attention did flag: a flock of geese out-side in the courtyard proved to be too much for his absorp-tion in the Hebrew alphabet.

But even this dirty and fetid hole had some redeeming features. 'There was one teacher whom I remember better than all others. He had a red beard, a very long red beard, which he used to stroke rhythmically all through the lesson, and very pale blue eyes with an innocent childish expression of wonderment. His gaze was always fixed on one corner of the ceiling, somewhere at the farthest end of the room, behind all the boys. He was telling and re-telling the story of the flight from Egypt. But he embroidered on it at will. His powerful imagination was bringing into our stuffy classroom the air and the smell and the breath of the Red Sea. We could feel the gentleness of the breeze that was moving forward the pillar of cloud. And the pillar of fire was glowing before our very eyes and the flames were dart-ing and dancing and breaking up into cascades of sparkling stars. But soon terrible fear gripped us all because we could hear the horses and chariots of the Pharaoh's army behind us. The tension was mounting and it seemed that in another minute we, "the children of Israel", would raise a loud cry "unto the Lord". But then, mercifully, we saw over our heads the stretched hand of Moses and under our feet there was the reassuring dry and firm land. The strong east wind was blowing the sea away. We were safe again between the waters "that were a wall" unto us. And the wall was truly magnificent: made of pure crystal with all the colours of the rainbow refracted and multiplied a thousandfold. We sat spellbound and hardly able to breathe.'

This kind of Jewish imagination nourished and stimulated Isaac in his childhood; and he remembered it with a strong and vivid sentiment. In his essay on the art of Marc Chagall he reaches down to the Jewish roots in some measure common to them both. Chagall in his youth transgressed against the rabbinical orthodoxy which 'stunted the growth of the visual arts'. 'For a Jew to paint was to rise in revolt, to achieve an act of emancipation'. Isaac achieved his act of emancipation by revolting against the Messianic faith and Khassidic tradition and going over to revolutionary socialism. It was the '*kheder* boy' in the great artist, the Jewish child who looks on the world with misty eyes full of wonder and fever that attracted Isaac to the early paintings of Chagall. The fantasy of the Yiddish folklore, as opposed to the rigidity of the orthodox religion, the poetry of those 'red-bearded' poor teachers who every day witnessed the crossing of the Red Sea, the songs of the bards, paupers, homeless singers and fiddlers, and above all, Jewish humour, were a never-failing source of fascination. It was characteristic and significant, he remarked, that nearly all the jokes on which Freud based his *Wit and the Unconscious* were Jewish jokes, full of self-mockery and self-irony, and just a whiff of self-pity. It was this humour that helped the persecuted and oppressed to bear the uncertainty and grimness of existence.

It was precisely the precariousness of this existence that became painfully obvious to Isaac, when as a boy he lived through the pogrom of Jews in his native Chrzanów. He suddenly became aware of the full force of hostility from his non-Jewish environment. True, it was a gentile friend of his father who came to warn the family of the impending disaster; but very few Jews had such friends and protectors. 'We lived in the centre of the town, in its richer and more bourgeois part, and not all our neighbours were Jews. Our front garden was tended with care and full of rose bushes and trees. On the ground floor was my father's printing shop and our living quarters were on the next floor. My father decided to barricade all windows and doors and to offer resistance to the attackers, should they try to break in. He stood behind the bolted door, armed with an iron rod which he brought from the cellar. All lights were out. We heard shouts and cries and the tumult of the approaching mob. The shrieks and cries for help or pity became louder and louder. Through the chinks in the shutters we could see the glow of distant flames. Were they going to set the whole town on fire? I sat petrified on the little steps which led from my parents' bedroom to my room. In a whisper I was reciting my prayers and I was clutching feverishly at the strings of my short *Tales* which I always wore over my shirt. The enraged mob was passing us by, though we could hear the breaking of windows in the house next door.'

Isaac was not yet eleven years old. His religious faith was already somewhat weakening. Yet in the hour of peril the strings of his orthodox dress, with their supposed powers to ward off evil, still seemed to him endowed with some magical qualities.

The wild destructive mob passed the Deutschers' house. But the experience was indelible. 'Next morning we ran away. We reached the railway station through streets littered with broken furniture, broken glass, charred books, smouldering bedding. When we arrived at the neighbouring little town, we were again confronted by anxious faces of local Jews. There were rumours that the peasants from the surrounding countryside were in an ugly mood.' Big market days were at the best of times occasions for a 'fight with the Yid'. The peasants used to seal every protracted commercial transaction with no less protracted drinking bouts. Vodka or home-brewed spirit would flow freely and soon any weapon—a long knife, a scythe, a club, or a horse-whip would be useful to settle accounts from the past or perhaps even any that might arise in the future. To the usual excitement of the market day now, in November 1918, was added the fervour of the new patriotism so skilfully and passionately preached from all churches in the re-gained Motherland.

The refugees from the Chrzanów pogrom moved farther, but the next town did not offer them security either. 'I lived through three pogroms during the very first week of reborn Poland,' recalled Isaac both in anger and sorrow. 'This is how the dawn of Polish independence greeted us.'

'1918 was the great year of my childhood,' he used to say. 'We lived in the so-called corner of three Emperors. On one side there was Russian Poland, on the other German Poland, and we were set right in the middle of that multi-racial population which constituted the Austro-Hungarian Empire. In this corner of the Three Emperors the year 1918 must have seemed even more dramatic than anywhere else in Europe. In that year all three monarchies collapsed and we lived through the landslide of three revolutions.'

Of that year Isaac had most vivid memories, and he was fond of recalling one particular incident which he saw as his first important lesson in politics. At the market place of Chrzanów, not far from the house of the Deutschers, stood the most impressive municipal building in the district. It was Town Hall and Police Station all in one. Over its heavy entrance door, on the big shield, was blazoned the emblem of the Habsburg Empire: a large eagle with wings spread and two heads, both crowned, looking left and right. One November day in 1918 a crowd of people gathered outside the Town Hall to talk about the latest proclamation of the last of the Habsburgs. A young boy, a hunchback, one of the least remarkable characters of the town, was climbing a long flimsy ladder placed against the roof of the municipal building. The whole crowd watched his swift movements with bated breath. He reached the flagpole and then the double-headed eagle. With two or three strokes of a hammer he loosened the shield from its base; then he looked down and shouted to the people below: 'Hey, there, step aside, take care!' The crowd moved back a little. The hunchback threw the Austrian eagle straight on the cobblestones of the square. The shield and eagle smashed into a hundred pieces. Next day a new flag, the Polish flag, was flying over Chrzanów.

The symbolism of the scene engraved itself on the memory of the future historian. When the moment comes, 'the least remarkable' hunchback of the little town can smash to bits the most awe-inspiring and revered imperial eagle.

\* \* \*

Isaac's childhood was coming to a close. Up to the age of thirteen he was attending the primary state school more or less regularly. After early morning prayers at the Synagogue he returned home, and then, by eight o'clock, plunged into the different world of the highly patriotic and highly religious Roman Catholic State school. 'We, Jewish boys, were allowed, indeed we were expected, to leave the classroom when the priest entered it for the daily lessons of Catholic religion. Although we rarely experienced any conscious anti-semitism on the part of our fellow pupils, after these particular lessons one could often detect a certain tension between the Christian boys and all those left outside the class. We were somehow made to feel the collective guilt for the drama of crucifixion. No words were uttered, but glances were disturbing. This mood did not last long, however; common games on the playground united us again.'

After school hours, in the afternoon, when most of Isaac's schoolmates did their homework or roamed the nearby fields, he went for his rabbinical studies. 'I suppose that the two orthodoxies—the morning Catholic one and the Jewish one—neutralized and cancelled each other in my thinking; very early I rejected them both and became an atheist', he said nearly half a century later.[1]

At thirteen in the life of the youngest of consecrated rabbis, the brilliant first pupil of the local Roman Catholic school, the budding writer and poet, a new phase began, full of strains and stresses. To the malaise of adolescence was now added a clearly defined rebellion against his Jewish religious education and against the chains of orthodoxy. A long process of 'bargaining with father' started: How many hours a day should he spend in the Synagogue? How many in the religious school? How many in the Polish *gymnasium*, the secondary school?

'I used to dream about the gymnasium. Everything

---

[1] Interviewed by German Television in July 1967.

seemed so attractive there: the modern, light and airy building covered with vineleaves; a large playground; the teachers, some of whom I knew already; but above all I longed
to wear the school uniform. I saw myself as a real student
with shining buttons on my jacket and a satchel full of books
—all, of course, about Polish poetry and history.' But this
dream was never to come true. There was no question of
allowing the boy who was the pride of the Jewish learned
community to waste his time on Polish secular education.
'With threats of suicide, with tears of despair, by using
logical intellectual arguments about the importance of all
and any education which I was convinced swayed my father,
we arrived at some sort of a compromise. We worked out a
timetable, a very unsatisfactory one for me. I was to give my
mornings and afternoons to the study of the Torah and the
Talmud, but I was to be allowed to follow in my own free
time the curriculum of the gymnasium. I was to be allowed
to keep in touch with the boys and the teachers and prepare
myself to sit for the examination as an extra-mural student.
My father had such an exaggerated idea of my abilities and
such a contempt for lay Polish education that, shrugging his
shoulders, he said: "You do not need more than two weeks
of work to learn all that over which the other boys sweat
the whole year round." '

Neither father nor son stuck, as fathers and sons seldom
do, to the bargain for very long. Isaac more and more often
deserted the Synagogue and the Jewish school for the light
and airy building of the gymnasium. He did not attend any
classes regularly. From time to time he sneaked into the
classroom of Professor Urbańczyk, the teacher of Polish
literature, who welcomed the curious little boy in a black
*kapota*, with his sidelocks clumsily hidden behind his ears.

Isaac used to enliven the lessons. He was full of ideas, bursting with questions, arguments, disagreements. When called upon, he would stand up, 'collect his thoughts' and deliver an original analysis of the subject or his own appreciation of the work of some Polish poet. He also organized a literary circle which used to meet out of school hours to discuss not only literary but also philosophical problems.

Here, however, a small scandal soon blew up. At one of the meetings Isaac opened a debate on a theme of his own choice: 'Christ was a Jew and a communist'. He started his speech, but was unable to continue; some boys were shocked, some terrified at the audacity of the Jew. 'All of a sudden I became an intruder, a stranger, I became a "Yid". Were they not taught at their lessons of religion, perhaps the same morning, that Jews murdered Christ? The two or three Jewish boys quietly left our gathering. Some, non-Jews, defended me, others were so incensed by my blasphemy that it all nearly ended in a fight.' The next day the whole school was in an uproar. The headmaster and teachers, who up to that time had tolerated Isaac's irregular and only semi-authorized incursions into the classroom, threatened to bar him altogether. It was the gentle Professor Urbańczyk who came to the rescue. He soothed tempers and finally hushed up the affair.

Very soon afterwards, however, the threat to Isaac's freelance attendance at school came from a different quarter. Jacob Deutscher decided that it was time for his son to leave the paternal home and devote himself to more serious theological studies which could not be pursued in the Chrzanów backwater. He was to benefit from the company of holy men and immerse himself thoroughly in the atmosphere of learned religious disputations. Jacob arranged to send his son to the Court of the Tsadik of Gere. This was a harsh blow to Isaac. He refused to go; he quarrelled bitterly with his father; he enlisted the support of his mother; and, finally, in despair, he cut short his sidelocks.

'This was not a gesture of defiance, but of utter desperation. That a Jew should appear at the Tsadik's Court without his *Peyes* (sidelocks) was unthinkable. I was convinced that my father would not expose himself to this shame, that he would be forced to give in, or at least to abandon the idea for some time. I was mistaken. My father looked at me. At first calmly, then with resentment, and then I could see terrible anger swelling up in him. He slapped me across my face. It was the first and only time that he had ever hit me. It was also the first and only time I saw a glint of fanaticism in his eyes.' Jacob Deutscher, torn between recurring religious doubts and strict orthodoxy, yearning for wider horizons and afraid of stepping beyond Judaism, was probably passing through a phase of religious passion which lit the spark of fanaticism in his eyes. Next day father and son set out on the pilgrimage: 'I resigned myself to my fate. My stratagem had not saved me. I was, of course, fully aware of the enormity of my offence: it is a sin for a Jew "to touch his sidelocks with a blade". I had burdened my father with my sin. I was full of pity for myself and full of pity for him for I knew how deeply I had hurt him.'

Isaac's stay at Gere did not, however, last long. Later in life he used to dismiss this experience with a shrug of the shoulders: 'I was plunged in the middle ages. My co-religionists lived as if in a trance—there was so much fervour and passion in their prayers and in their ritual. But there was also a handful of rich Jews who were much less zealous in their observance of the rites. They used to come on short visits, some of them from abroad, to seek the Tsadik's wise advice on their business affairs. Some of them were quite cynical: they were offering the "saintly man" a share in their business transactions; in return he gave them his blessing which they treated as a form of spiritual re-insurance.'

After only two or three weeks Jacob Deutscher brought his son back home. The phase of fanaticism was over, and now into the relationship of father and son, reconciled and perhaps both a little remorseful, entered a fresh note of warmth and affection. The long winter evenings were again devoted to common reading. It was in the choice of reading matter that the conflict in the mind of the father used to show itself most clearly. Upon his return from the archaic and stifling atmosphere of Gere, with its scholastic teaching and thirteenth-century way of life, Isaac was set the task of studying the works of Goethe and Lessing or the philosophical treatises of Spinoza. Every page of the books which his father read with him proclaimed: *de omnibus dubitandum*; yet a few weeks back, at the Court of the Wonderrabbi, all was tradition, authority, and blind faith. Spinoza the rebel, the atheist, the heretic, the excommunicated Jew, proved an all too successful mentor for the very young rabbi who was already abandoning religion for good and all.

When father and son were in a lighter mood they used to turn to Heine's poetry and prose. Here again the *History of Religion in Germany*, which Isaac knew almost by heart, could not lead back to the Synagogue, but away from it. Then there were the evenings when Heine's lyrics and poems and satirical verses were read aloud. The reciting of the long poem '*Disputation*', in which a Catholic priest and a Jewish rabbi debate the worth and value of their respective religions, was the cause of great merriment. The poem ends thus:

> *Welcher recht hat weiss ich nicht—*
> *Doch es will mich schier bedünken,*
> *Dass der Rabbi und der Mönch,*
> *Dass sie alle beide stinken.*

No wonder that next morning and for a few days afterwards Isaac's place in the Synagogue remained empty.

\* \* \*

'Spinoza, Heine, Lassalle . . . these are your three heroes', Isaac used to tell his father, 'you are pushing their works into my hands, you read them with me and you are passing on to me your enthusiasm for their philosophy and their ideas. All three of them left Judaism and religion or transcended it. And you want me to remain true and faithful to what already for Spinoza in the seventeenth century was an anachronism and for Heine and Lassalle nearly a hundred years ago was ridiculous. You want me to accept meekly the life you mapped out for me and yet all your heroes were rebels, apostates, subverters.'

There is no doubt that Jacob Deutscher was the greatest single influence in Isaac's childhood and adolescence. There was a harmony and intellectual communion between father and son which allowed them to understand each other; there was also discord and disagreement, which made their relations at times stormy, painful, but always rich and highly charged. In this relationship the son's personality formed itself.

This is how Isaac, a month before his death, saw his father:[1] 'My father was an orthodox Jew, in love with

[1] Interviewed by German Television.

German culture, philosophy, and poetry . . . He was always wanting to read German literature and German periodicals with me. He had himself, in his youth, published essays in the *Neue Freie Presse*, the best-known Viennese newspaper; had been correspondent of the Warsaw *Haʒefira*, the first daily to appear in the Hebrew language; and had also written a little book in Hebrew about Spinoza, with the Latin title *Amor Dei Intellectualis*. Spinoza was one of his heroes; Heine the other. My father also had a great respect for Lassalle, but the highest intellectual ideal for him, apart from Hebrew writers, was, of course, Goethe. I did not share my father's partiality for German poetry. I was a Polish patriot. Mickiewicz and Słowacki were incomparably dearer and closer to me. For this reason I never learned the German language thoroughly either.[1] My father often used to say to me: "Yes, you want to write all your fine poetry only in Polish. I know you will be a great writer one day"—for my father had quite an exaggerated idea of my literary talent, and wanted me to exercise it in a "world language". "German", he would say, "is *the* world language. Why should you bury all your talent in a provincial language? You have only to go beyond Auschwitz . . ."—Auschwitz was just near us, on the frontier—"you have only to go beyond Auschwitz, and practically nobody will understand you any more, you and your fine Polish language. You really must learn German." That was his ever-recurring refrain: "You have only to go beyond Auschwitz and you will be totally lost, my son!" Impatient as I was, I often interrupted him: "I already know what you are going to say, father—You have only to go beyond Auschwitz, and you will be lost." The tragic truth is that my father never

---

[1] Isaac spoke a fluent and idiomatic German.

went beyond Auschwitz. During the second World War he disappeared into Auschwitz.'

Isaac did indeed reconcile himself to German language and culture in the end: what brought this about were the works of Marx and Engels. But these he read much, much later, as an adult. 'I was a Polish child, brought up in a Polish school. For us the Germans, like the Russians, were oppressors who robbed us of our independence for a century and a half, and against whom we had struggled in numerous insurrections. In school we sang the song of Maria Konopnicka, a great and celebrated poetess, with the following refrain: "The German will not spit in our faces, nor will he make Germans of our children". And here was my father wanting to "make a German" of me! This attempt went against all my sensitivity to Polish lyrical poetry and all my romantic notions of Polish independence.'

*        *        *

*Amor Dei Intellectualis* might have been the motto of both Jacob and Isaac Deutscher. This motto contradicted all the efforts of the father who aimed at a theological career for his firstborn. The father himself, indirectly and unwittingly, sowed all the seeds of doubt and planted in Isaac that respect for heresy which remained characteristically his till the end.

When, at what point in his life, did Isaac abandon religion for good and all? This was, of course, a gradual process. But there is no doubt that one particular episode, highly dramatic, which appealed to Isaac's sense of the theatrical, sealed the final break. Here again, though only remotely, the personality of Isaac's father contributed something to his son's development.

A few months after Isaac's fourteenth birthday he became very friendly with a young apprentice in the printing shop. An excellent worker, very mature for his age, always well informed about current political events, he was a communist and an atheist—and yet he was Jacob Deutscher's favourite! He treated Isaac with a little condescension and a touch of irony; but liked to engage him in all sorts of arguments about politics and religion. In both he seemed to be determined to convert Isaac to his views. On the eve of Yom Kippur, the Day of Atonement, he 'dared' Isaac: 'If you really do not believe in God, he said, prove it. Come and meet me tomorrow at the gate to the Jewish cemetery.' Isaac agreed. While his parents were at prayers, the two met. The apprentice led the younger boy to the grave of a rabbi. There he took out of his pocket a couple of sandwiches with butter and ham. This was, indeed, blasphemy multiplied a thousandfold; it was piling sin upon sin. On the day of the most solemn fast, when not even a drop of water should pass the lips of the orthodox Jew, Isaac was handed the most sinful of food. The mere sight of ham should have been odious to him; to put any meat between layers of butter was a grave offence against the ritual laws; here was ham, the most abhorrent, the most evil of messes. 'I was petrified by the iniquity of my behaviour. I munched the sandwich and swallowed each mouthful with difficulty. I half-hoped and half-feared that something terrible would happen; I waited for a thunder that would strike me down. But nothing happened. All was quiet. My companion treated the whole experiment as a huge joke. He shook my hand and patted me approvingly on the back. I left him and ran back to the town.'

At the Synagogue nobody had noticed Isaac's absence.

He returned from the sinful escapade just in time to mix with the crowd of people who after the day of prayers and fasting were returning to their homes for a solemn feast.

'At the family table I could hardly lift my eyes. I have never felt more remorseful in all my life. Not for what I had done; it was not at all the offence against the Mosaic law that weighed so heavy on my conscience. The solicitude of my father, the tenderness of my mother, who, herself pale and worn out by the long fast, was hurrying to feed the hungry family—to feed me first of all—became unbearable.'

Isaac used to relate this episode with a great deal of emotion. The unholy meal on the grave of the rabbi, the sacrilege, the impiety, his own fears, faith and disbelief, were only the culmination of a long drawn process towards complete atheism. But on that evening it was not God who was mocked, but his parents who were deceived. That was what made the young offender choke with food, shame, and tears.

\*     \*     \*

Isaac did not live to describe his childhood, as he planned to do; but the autobiographical touches in so many of his works show what happened in his pilgrimage of belief. In the first essay of this volume he speaks indirectly about himself, his origin, his intellectual and philosophical development. He belongs, and he saw himself belonging, to that breed of non-Jewish Jews who transcended Judaism and went beyond Jewry to the highest ideals of mankind. Like Heine, Marx, Rosa Luxemburg, Trotsky, and Freud, Isaac found Jewry, and all religion, too constricting. Like them he lived on the borderlines of various national cultures and was in society—Polish, Jewish, German, English—and yet not of it. In this he was in the Jewish tradition, and he never denied it.

On the last evening of his life we viewed from the height of the Capitol the Arch of Titus, brightly illumined by the brilliant full moon of a summer night. In his precise, well-rounded English sentences, full of pathos and poetry, Isaac was telling us again how hated by the Jews was this symbol of Roman triumph.

'The battle for Jerusalem was protracted. Titus paraded his legions outside the walls of the besieged city. His cohorts were well armed and looked fierce and might have struck fear into the hearts of the besieged. You must remember', Isaac went on persuasively, 'that all around the Romans were already in possession of the whole country—Jerusalem stood alone. There was the Temple surrounded by walls; then there was the royal palace, also enclosed by fortifications. There were inner bulwarks, elaborately constructed defences, and outer fortifications. The defenders could venture out to harass their enemies; but they had to retreat again and again into their enormous and seemingly impregnable compound. And the Romans were impatient; and their pride was hurt, and they concentrated all their forces on the assault. Titus ordered them not to slacken their attacks. Inside the fortress there were over half a million men, women, and children, and all were armed and were not afraid of dying. And they saw the flash of lightning and they heard the voice of God telling them to defend the Temple to their last breath; and they did. But Titus was stronger; and he stormed the bastion with all his strength; and the walls crumbled. In Rome there was rejoicing. The Arch was built to commemorate the triumphal return of Titus and his troops from Judea. It marks the fall of Jerusalem and the destruction of the

Temple. Generations of Jews have been shedding tears and sighing at the thought of the calamity.'

More than half a century had passed since Isaac's imagination was stirred when he heard this tragic story from the lips of his teacher, the poetic visionary, red-bearded *rebe* of the Jewish school.

Isaac's road from the *kheder* of Chrzanów to the lecture halls of Cambridge and Harvard, to the Berkeley campus of rebelling students was very long; it was also solitary and arduous.

> 'The childhood shows the man
> As morning shows the day'

wrote Milton. It seems that Isaac obeyed Milton's behest:

> 'Be famous then
> By wisdom; as thy empire must extend,
> So let extend thy mind o'er all the world.'

*London, December* 1967          *Tamara Deutscher*

# I

# The non-Jewish Jew[1]

THERE is an old Talmudic saying: 'A Jew who has sinned still remains a Jew.' My own thinking is, of course, beyond the idea of 'sin' or 'no sin'; but this saying has brought to my mind a memory from childhood which may not be irrelevant to my theme.

I remember that when as a child I read the *Midrash*, I came across a story and a description of a scene which gripped my imagination. It was the story of Rabbi Meir, the great saint and sage, the pillar of Mosaic orthodoxy, and co-author of the *Mishnah*, who took lessons in theology from a heretic, Elisha ben Abiyuh, called Akher (The Stranger). Once on a Sabbath Rabbi Meir was with his teacher, and as usual they became engaged in a deep argument. The heretic was riding a donkey, and Rabbi Meir, as he could not ride on a Sabbath, walked by his side and listened so intently to the words of wisdom falling from his heretical lips that he failed to notice that he and his teacher had reached the ritual boundary which Jews were not allowed to cross on a Sabbath. The great heretic turned to his orthodox pupil and said: 'Look, we have reached the boundary—we must part now; you must not accompany

[1] This essay is based on a lecture given during Jewish Book Week to the World Jewish Congress, in February 1958.

me any farther—go back!' Rabbi Meir went back to the
Jewish community, while the heretic rode on—beyond the
boundaries of Jewry.

There was enough in this scene to puzzle an orthodox
Jewish child. Why, I wondered, did Rabbi Meir, that leading light of orthodoxy, take his lessons from the heretic?
Why did he show him so much affection? Why did he defend
him against other rabbis? My heart, it seems, was with the
heretic. Who was he? He appeared to be in Jewry and yet
out of it. He showed a curious respect for his pupil's orthodoxy, when he sent him back to the Jews on the Holy
Sabbath; but he himself, disregarding canon and ritual, rode
beyond the boundaries. When I was thirteen, or perhaps
fourteen, I began to write a play about Akher and Rabbi
Meir and I tried to find out more about Akher's character.
What made him transcend Judaism? Was he a Gnostic?
Was he an adherent of some other school of Greek or Roman
philosophy? I could not find the answers, and did not manage to get beyond the first act.

The Jewish heretic who transcends Jewry belongs to a
Jewish tradition. You may, if you like, see Akher as a pro-
totype of those great revolutionaries of modern thought:
Spinoza, Heine, Marx, Rosa Luxemburg, Trotsky, and
Freud. You may, if you wish to, place them within a Jewish
tradition. They all went beyond the boundaries of Jewry.
They all found Jewry too narrow, too archaic, and too constricting. They all looked for ideals and fulfilment beyond
it, and they represent the sum and substance of much that is
greatest in modern thought, the sum and substance of the
most profound upheavals that have taken place in philosophy,
sociology, economics, and politics in the last three centuries.

Did they have anything in common with one another? Have they perhaps impressed mankind's thought so greatly because of their special 'Jewish genius'? I do not believe in the exclusive genius of any race. Yet I think that in some ways they were very Jewish indeed. They had in themselves something of the quintessence of Jewish life and of the Jewish intellect. They were *a priori* exceptional in that as Jews they dwelt on the borderlines of various civilizations, religions, and national cultures. They were born and brought up on the borderlines of various epochs. Their mind matured where the most diverse cultural influences crossed and fertilized each other. They lived on the margins or in the nooks and crannies of their respective nations. Each of them was in society and yet not in it, of it and yet not of it. It was this that enabled them to rise in thought above their societies, above their nations, above their times and generations, and to strike out mentally into wide new horizons and far into the future.

It was, I think, an English Protestant biographer of Spinoza who said that only a Jew could have carried out that upheaval in the philosophy of his age that Spinoza carried out—a Jew who was not bound by the dogmas of the Christian Churches, Catholic and Protestant, nor by those of the faith in which he had been born.[1] Neither Descartes nor Leibnitz could free themselves to the same extent from the shackles of the medieval scholastical tradition in philosophy.

[1] 'It is a serious disadvantage resulting from the great outward triumph of Christianity that the thinkers of Christendom rarely come into vital contact with other religions and other modes of world orientation. The consequence of this inexperience is that Christian ways of looking at the world are assumed to be true as a matter of course. . . . The boldest and most original thinker . . . was Spinoza, who stood above the theological prejudices from which the others could not entirely extricate themselves.' (*The Correspondence of Spinoza*; Introduction by A. Wolf.)

Spinoza was brought up under the influences of Spain, Holland, Germany, England, and the Italy of the Renaissance—all the trends of human thought that were at work at that time shaped his mind. His native Holland was in the throes of bourgeois revolution. His ancestors, before they came to the Netherlands, had been Spanish-Portuguese *Maranim*, crypto-Jews, at heart Jews, outwardly Christian, as were many Spanish Jews on whom the Inquisition had forced the baptism. After the Spinozas had come to the Netherlands, they disclosed themselves as Jews; but, of course, neither they nor their close descendants were strangers to the intellectual climate of Christianity.

Spinoza himself, when he started out as independent thinker and as initiator of modern criticism of the Bible, seized at once the cardinal contradiction in Judaism, the contradiction between the monotheistic and universal God and the setting in which that God appears in the Jewish religion—as a God attached to one people only; the contradiction between the universal God and his 'chosen people'. We know what the realization of this contradiction brought upon Spinoza: banishment from the Jewish community and excommunication. He had to fight against the Jewish clergy which, itself recently a victim of the Inquisition, became infected with the spirit of the Inquisition. Then he had to face the hostility of the Catholic clergy and Calvinistic priests. His whole life was a struggle to overcome the limitations of the religions and cultures of his time.

Among Jews of great intellect exposed to the contradiction of various religions and cultures some were so pulled in various directions by contradictory influences and pressures that they could not find spiritual balance, and broke down. One of these was Uriel Acosta, Spinoza's elder and forerunner. Many times he rebelled against Judaism; and many times he recanted. The rabbis excommunicated him repeatedly; he repeatedly prostrated himself before them on the floor of the Amsterdam Synagogue. Unlike Acosta, Spinoza had the great intellectual happiness of being able to harmonize the conflicting influences and to create out of them a higher outlook on the world and an integrated philosophy.

In almost every generation, whenever the Jewish intellectual, placed at the concatenation of various cultures, struggles with himself and with the problems of his time, we find someone who, like Uriel Acosta, breaks down under the burden, and someone who, like Spinoza, makes of that burden the wings of his greatness. Heine was in a sense the Uriel Acosta of a later age. His relation to Marx, Spinoza's intellectual grandson, is comparable to Uriel Acosta's relation to Spinoza.

Heine was torn between Christianity and Jewry, and between France and Germany. In his native Rhineland there clashed the influences of the French Revolution and of the Napoleonic Empire with those of the old Holy Roman Empire of the German Kaisers. He grew up within the orbit of classical German philosophy and within the orbit of French Republicanism; and he saw Kant as a Robespierre and Fichte as a Napoleon in the realm of the spirit; and so he describes them in one of the most profound and moving passages of *Zur Geschichte der Religion and Philosophie in Deutschland*. In his later years he came in contact with French and German socialism and communism; and he met Marx with that apprehensive admiration and sympathy with which Acosta had met Spinoza.

Marx likewise grew up in the Rhineland. His parents

having ceased to be Jews, he did not struggle with the Jewish heritage as Heine did. All the more intense was his opposition to the social and spiritual backwardness of contemporary Germany. An exile most of his life, his thought was shaped by German philosophy, French socialism, and English political economy. In no other contemporary mind did such diverse influences meet so fruitfully. Marx rose above German philosophy, French socialism, and English political economy; he absorbed what was best in each of these trends and transcended the limitations of each.

To come nearer to our time, there were Rosa Luxemburg, Trotsky, and Freud, each of whom was formed amid historic cross-currents. Rosa Luxemburg is a unique blend of the German, Polish, and Russian characters and of the Jewish temperament; Trotsky was the pupil of a Lutheran Russo-German gymnasium in cosmopolitan Odessa on the fringe of the Greek-Orthodox Empire of the Tsars; and Freud's mind matured in Vienna in estrangement from Jewry and in opposition to the Catholic clericalism of the Habsburg capital. All of them had this in common, that the very conditions in which they lived and worked did not allow them to reconcile themselves to ideas which were nationally or religiously limited and induced them to strive for a universal *Weltanschauung*.

Spinoza's ethics were no longer the Jewish ethics, but the ethics of man at large—just as his God was no longer the Jewish God: his God, merged with nature, shed his separate and distinctive divine identity. Yet, in a way, Spinoza's God and ethics were still Jewish, except that his was Jewish monotheism carried to its logical conclusion and the Jewish universal God thought out to the end; and once thought out to the end, that God ceased to be Jewish.

Heine wrestled with Jewry all his life; his attitude towards it was characteristically ambivalent, full of love-hate or hate-love. He was in this respect inferior to Spinoza, who, excommunicated by the Jews, did not become a Christian. Heine did not have Spinoza's strength of mind and character; and he lived in a society which even in the first decades of the nineteenth century was still more backward than Dutch society had been in the seventeenth. At first he pinned his hopes on that pseudo-emancipation of Jews, the ideal which Moses Mendelsohn had expressed in the words: 'be a Jew inside your home and a man outside.' The timidity of that German-Jewish ideal was of a piece with the paltry liberalism of the gentile German bourgeoisie: the German Liberal was a 'free man' inside his home and an *allertreuester Untertane* ('the most faithful subject') outside. This could not satisfy Heine for long. He abandoned Jewry and surrendered to Christianity. At heart he was never reconciled to the abandonment and the conversion. His rejection of Jewish orthodoxy runs through the whole of his work. His Don Isaac says to the Rabbi von Bachrach: 'I could not be one of you. I like your cooking much better than I like your religion. No, I could not be one of you; and I suspect that even at the best of times, under the rule of your King David, in the best of your times, I would have run away from you and gone to the temples of Assyria and Babylon which were full of love and the joy of life.' Yet, it was a fiery and resentful Jew who had, in *An Edom*, '*gewaltig beschworen den tausendjährigen Schmerz.*'

Marx, about twenty years younger, surmounted the problem which tormented Heine. Only once did he come to grips with it, in his youthful and famous *Zur Judenfrage*. This was his unreserved rejection of Jewry. Apologists of

Jewish orthodoxy and Jewish nationalism have because of it violently attacked Marx as an 'anti-Semite'. Yet, I think that Marx went to the very heart of the matter when he said that Jewry had survived 'not in spite of history but in history and through history', that it owed its survival to the distinctive role that the Jews had played as agents of a money economy in environments which lived in a natural economy; that Judaism was essentially a theoretical epitome of market relationships and the faith of the merchant; and that Christian Europe, as it developed from feudalism to capitalism, became Jewish in a sense. Marx saw Christ as the 'theorizing Jew', the Jew as a 'practical Christian' and, therefore, the 'practical' bourgeois Christian as a 'Jew'. Since he treated Judaism as the religious reflection of the bourgeois way of thought, he saw bourgeois Europe as becoming assimilated to Jewry. His ideal was not the equality of Jew and Gentile in a 'Judaized' capitalist society, but the emancipation of Jew and non-Jew alike from the bourgeois way of life, or, as he put it provocatively in his somewhat over-paradoxical Young Hegelian idiom, in the 'emancipation of society from Jewry'. His idea was as universal as Spinoza's, yet advanced in time by two hundred years—it was the idea of socialism and of the classless and stateless society.

Among Marx's many disciples and followers hardly any were, in spirit and temperament, as close to him as Rosa Luxemburg and Leon Trotsky. Their affinity with him shows itself in their dialectically dramatic vision of the world and of its class struggles, and in that exceptional concord of thought, passion, and imagination which gives to their language and style a peculiar clarity, density, and richness. (Bernard Shaw had probably these qualities in mind when he spoke of Marx's 'peculiarly Jewish literary gifts'.) Like Marx, Rosa Luxemburg and Trotsky strove, together with their non-Jewish comrades, for the universal, as against the particularist, and for the internationalist, as against the nationalist, solutions to the problems of their time. Rosa Luxemburg sought to transcend the contradiction between German reformist socialism and Russian revolutionary Marxism. She sought to inject into German socialism something of the Russian and Polish revolutionary *élan* and idealism, something of that 'revolutionary romanticism' which so great a realist as Lenin unabashingly extolled; and occasionally she tried to transplant the Western European democratic spirit and tradition into the socialist underground movements of Eastern Europe. She failed in her main purpose and paid with her life. But it was not only she who paid. In her assassination Hohenzollern Germany celebrated its last triumph and Nazi Germany—its first.

Trotsky, the author of permanent revolution, had before him the vision of a global upheaval transforming mankind. The leader, together with Lenin, of the Russian revolution and the founder of the Red Army, he came in conflict with the State he had helped to create when that State and its leaders put up the banner of Socialism in One Country. Not for him was the limitation of the vision of socialism to the boundaries of one country.

All these great revolutionaries were extremely vulnerable. They were, as Jews, rootless, in a sense; but they were so only in some respects, for they had the deepest roots in intellectual tradition and in the noblest aspirations of their times. Yet whenever religious intolerance or nationalist emotion was on the ascendant, whenever dogmatic narrow-mindedness and fanaticism triumphed, they were the first victims. They were excommunicated by Jewish rabbis; they were persecuted by Christian priests; they were hunted down by the gendarmes of absolute rulers and by the *soldateska*; they were hated by pseudo-democratic philistines; and they were expelled by their own parties. Nearly all of them were exiled from their countries; and the writings of all were burned at the stake at one time or another. Spinoza's name could not be mentioned for over a century after his death—even Leibnitz, who was indebted to Spinoza for so much of his thought, did not dare to mention it. Trotsky is still under anathema in Russia today. The names of Marx, Heine, Freud, and Rosa Luxemburg were forbidden in Germany quite recently. But theirs is the ultimate victory. After a century during which Spinoza's name was covered with oblivion, they put up monuments to him and acknowledged him as the greatest fructifier of the human mind. Herder once said about Goethe: 'I wish Goethe read some Latin books apart from Spinoza's *Ethics*.' Goethe was indeed steeped in Spinoza's thought; and Heine rightly describes him as 'Spinoza who has thrown off the cloak of his geometrical-mathematical formulae and stands before us as a lyrical poet.' Heine himself has triumphed over Hitler and Goebbels. The other revolutionaries of this line will also survive and sooner or later triumph over those who have worked hard to efface their memory.

It is very obvious why Freud belongs to the same intellectual line. In his teachings, whatever their merits and demerits, he transcends the limitations of earlier psychological schools. The man whom he analyses is not a German, or an Englishman, a Russian, or a Jew—he is the universal man in whom the subconscious and the conscious struggle, the man who is part of nature and part of society, the man whose desires and cravings, scruples and inhibitions, anxieties and predicaments are essentially the same no matter to what race, religion, or nation he belongs. From their viewpoint the Nazis were right when they coupled Freud's name with that of Marx and burned the books of both.

All these thinkers and revolutionaries have had certain philosophical principles in common. Although their philosophies vary, of course, from century to century and from generation to generation, they are all, from Spinoza to Freud, determinists, they all hold that the universe is ruled by laws inherent in it and governed by *Gesetzmässigkeiten*. They do not see reality as a jumble of accidents or history as an assemblage of caprices and whims of rulers. There is nothing fortuitous, so Freud tells us, in our dreams, follies, or even in our slips of the tongue. The laws of development, Trotsky says, 'refract' themselves through accidents; and in saying this he is very close to Spinoza.

They are all determinists because having watched many societies and studied many 'ways of life' at close quarters, they grasp the basic regularities of life. Their manner of thinking is dialectical, because, living on borderlines of nations and religions, they see society in a state of flux. They conceive reality as being dynamic, not static. Those who are shut in within one society, one nation, or one religion, tend to imagine that their way of life and their way of thought have absolute and unchangeable validity and that all that contradicts their standards is somehow 'unnatural', inferior, or evil. Those, on the other hand, who live on the borderlines of various civilizations comprehend more clearly the great movement and the great contradictoriness of nature and society.

All these thinkers agree on the relativity of moral standards. None of them believes in absolute good or absolute evil. They all observed communities adhering to different moral standards and different ethical values. What was good to the Roman Catholic Inquisition under which Spinoza's grandparents had lived, was evil to the Jews; and what was good to the rabbis and Jewish elders of Amsterdam was evil to Spinoza himself. Heine and Marx experienced in their youth the tremendous clash between the morality of the French revolution and that of feudal Germany.

Nearly all these thinkers have yet another great philosophical idea in common—the idea that knowledge to be real must be active. This incidentally has a bearing on their views on ethics, for if knowledge is inseparable from action or *Praxis*, which is by its nature relative and self-contradictory, then morality, the knowledge of what is good and what is evil, is also inseparable from *Praxis* and is also relative and self-contradictory. It was Spinoza who said that 'to be is to do and to know is to do'. It was only one step from this to Marx's saying that 'hitherto the philosophers have interpreted the world; henceforth the task is to change it'.

Finally, all these men, from Spinoza to Freud, believed in the ultimate solidarity of man; and this was implicit in their attitudes towards Jewry. We are now looking back on these believers in humanity through the bloody fog of our times. We are looking back at them through the smoke of the gas chambers, the smoke which no wind can disperse from our sight. These 'non-Jewish Jews' were essentially optimists; and their optimism reached heights which it is not easy to ascend in our times. They did not imagine that it would be possible for 'civilized' Europe in the twentieth century to sink to a depth of barbarity at which the mere words 'solidarity of man' would sound as a perverse mockery to Jewish ears. Alone among them Heine had the poet's intuitive premonition of this when he warned Europe to beware of the coming onslaught of the old Germanic gods emerging '*aus dem teutschem Urwalde*', and when he complained that the destiny of the modern Jew is tragic beyond expression and comprehension—so tragic that 'they laugh at you when you speak of it, and this is the greatest tragedy of all.'

We do not find this premonition in Spinoza or Marx. Freud in his old age reeled mentally under the blow of Nazism. To Trotsky it came as a shock that Stalin used against him the anti-semitic innuendo. As a young man Trotsky had, in most categorical terms, repudiated the demand for Jewish 'cultural autonomy', which the *Bund*, the Jewish Socialist Party, raised in 1903. He did it in the name of the solidarity of Jew and non-Jew in the socialist camp. Nearly a quarter of a century later, while he was engaged in an unequal struggle with Stalin and went to the party cells in Moscow to expound his views, he was met with vicious allusions to his Jewishness and even with plain anti-semitic insults. The allusions and insults came from members of the party which he had, together with Lenin, led in the revolution and civil war. After another quarter of a century, and after Auschwitz and Majdanek and Belsen, once again, this time much more openly and menacingly, Stalin resorted to anti-semitic innuendo and insult.

It is an indubitable fact that the Nazi massacre of six million European Jews has not made any deep impression on the nations of Europe. It has not truly shocked their conscience. It has left them almost cold. Was then the optimistic belief in humanity voiced by the great Jewish revolutionaries justified? Can we still share their faith in the future of civilization?

I admit that if one were to try and answer these questions from an exclusively Jewish standpoint, it would be hard, perhaps impossible, to give a positive answer. As for myself, I cannot approach the issue from an exclusively Jewish standpoint; and my answer is: Yes, their faith was justified. It was justified at any rate, in so far as the belief in the ultimate solidarity of mankind is itself one of the conditions necessary for the preservation of humanity and for the cleansing of our civilization of the dregs of barbarity that are still present in it and still poison it.

Why then has the fate of the European Jews left the nations of Europe, or the gentile world at large, almost cold? Unfortunately, Marx was far more right about the place of the Jews in European society than we could have realized some time ago. The major part of the Jewish tragedy has consisted in this, that as the result of a long historic development, the masses of Europe have become accustomed to identify the Jew primarily with trade and jobbing, money-lending and money-making. Of these the Jew had become the synonym and symbol to the popular mind. Look up the Oxford English Dictionary and see how it gives the accepted meaning of the term 'Jew': firstly, it is a 'person of the Hebrew race'; secondly—this is the colloquial use—an 'extortionate usurer, driver of hard bargains.' 'Rich as a Jew' says the proverb. Colloquially the word is also used as a transitive verb: to jew, the Oxford Dictionary tells us, means to 'cheat, overreach'. This is the vulgar image of the Jew and the vulgar prejudice against him, fixed in many languages, not only in English, and in many works of art, not only in *The Merchant of Venice*.

However, this is not only the vulgar image. Remember what was the occasion on which Macaulay pleaded, and the manner in which he pleaded, for political equality of Jew and gentile and for the Jew's right to sit in the House of Commons. The occasion was the admission to the House of a Rothschild, the first Jew to sit in the House, the Jew elected as Member for the City of London. And Macaulay's argument was this: if we allow the Jew to manage our financial affairs for us, why should we not allow him to sit among us here, in Parliament, and have a say in the management of all our public affairs? This was the voice of the bourgeois Christian who took a fresh look at Shylock and hailed him as brother.

I suggest that what had enabled the Jews to survive as a separate community, the fact that they had represented the market economy amidst people living in a natural economy—that this fact and its popular memories have also been responsible, at least in part, for the *Schadenfreude* or the indifference with which the populace of Europe has witnessed the holocaust of the Jews. It has been the misfortune of the Jews that, when the nations of Europe turned against capitalism, they did so only very superficially, at any rate in the first half of this century. They attacked not the core of capitalism, not its productive relationship, not its organization of property and labour, but its externals and its largely archaic trappings which so often were indeed Jewish. This is the crux of the Jewish tragedy. Decaying capitalism has overstayed its day and has morally dragged down mankind; and we, the Jews, have paid for it and may yet have to pay for it.

All this has driven the Jews to see their own State as *the* way out. Most of the great revolutionaries, whose heritage I am discussing, have seen the ultimate solution to the problems of their and our times not in nation-states but in international society. As Jews they were the natural pioneers of this idea, for who was as well qualified to preach the international society of equals as were the Jews free from all Jewish and non-Jewish orthodoxy and nationalism?

However, the decay of bourgeois Europe has compelled the Jew to embrace the nation state. This is the paradoxical consummation of the Jewish tragedy. It is paradoxical, because we live in an age when the nation-state is fast becoming an anachronism, and an archaism—not only the nation-state of Israel but the nation-states of Russia, the United States, Great Britain, France, Germany, and others. They are all anachronisms. Do you not see this yet? Is it not clear that at a time when atomic energy daily reduces the globe in size, when man has started out on his interplanetary journey, when a sputnik flies over the territory of a great nation-state in a minute or in seconds, that at such a time technology renders the nation-state as ridiculous and out-lived as little medieval princedoms were in the age of the steam-engine?

Even those young nation-states that have come into being as the result of a necessary and progressive struggle waged by colonial and semi-colonial peoples for emancipation—India, Burma, Ghana, Algeria, and others—cannot preserve their progressive character for long. They form a necessary stage in the history of some peoples; but it is a stage that those peoples too will have to overcome in order to find wider frameworks for their existence. In our epoch any new nation-state, soon after its constitution, begins to be affected by the general decline of this form of political organization; and this is already showing itself in the short experience of India, Ghana, and Israel.

The world has compelled the Jew to embrace the nation-state and to make of it his pride and hope just at a time when there is little or no hope left in it. You cannot blame the Jews for this; you must blame the world. But Jews should at least be aware of the paradox and realize that their intense enthusiasm for 'national sovereignty' is historically belated. They did not benefit from the advantages of the nation-state in those centuries when it was a medium of mankind's advance and a great revolutionary and unifying factor in history. They have taken possession of it only after it had become a factor of disunity and social disintegration.

I hope, therefore, that, together with other nations, the Jews will ultimately become aware—or regain the aware-ness—of the inadequacy of the nation-state and that they will find their way back to the moral and political heritage that the genius of the Jews who have gone beyond Jewry has left us—the message of universal human emancipation.

# II

# Who is a Jew?[1]

THE fact that the question 'Who is a Jew?' can be posed at all gives me an uncanny feeling that I am about to discuss one of the familiar topics of so many modern novels from Kafka to Nigel Dennis: lost identity cards, or perhaps some that are *introuvables*.

When so many intellectuals reject the rituals, the taboos, the do's and don't's of any religion, how can one expect a Jewish intellectual to identify himself with the accepted, archaic orthodox Jewish traditions? Some thirty years ago I should have thought that the question 'What makes the identity of a Jew, of a Jewish intellectual?' was completely irrelevant, and I partly think so now too. It is not enough to ask the question about the identity of an abstract Jewish intellectual, nor is it fruitful to speak of him as if he were the manifestation of that great EGO—in capital letters—which exists in some sort of a vacuum of a Jewish eternity. The

---

[1] 'Who is a Jew? What is the place of the Jewish intellectual in modern society and what role should he play in it?' These questions were in the heart of a lively debate going on in Jewish circles in the mid-1960s. Isaac Deutscher's contribution took the form of an interview given to *The Jewish Quarterly* (London, 1966) in which he questioned the tacit assumption of the existence of a positive 'Jewish community'; he also took part in a discussion sponsored by the British Section of the World Jewish Congress in November 1963. This essay is a condensed version of the interview and his intervention in the discussion.

identity of the Jewish intellectual—yes, but in what world, in what environment, in what relationship to the problems of our time? This is how, I feel, one should pose the question if one poses it at all.

It is too unreal and futile to concern oneself solely and exclusively with the solipsism of the Jewish intellectual trying to define himself without much reference to the outside world, and to the antagonisms by which it is rent and by which mankind is divided. If we are also concerned with the place of the Jew in society, we must immediately inquire what Jew we have in mind and what kind of society we are thinking of. The Jew in American or in Soviet society? In Britain? In France? In Germany or in Israel? In each of these societies the position of the Jew is different. What common denominator is there between the attitudes, roles and functions of Jews in such different circumstances?

It is highly significant and characteristic of our epoch that now more than ever before the Jew feels the urge to try to define his position *vis-à-vis* his non-Jewish environment. He knows that his role is different in quality from the role, say, of the Irish intellectual in the United States. Did President Kennedy ever inquire into his identity as an Irish intellectual? And yet the Jew is always aware, painfully aware, that there is a tremendous difference between his position and that of the Irishman in America. He somehow feels that in the Great Democracy he is 'the other' Negro: a white-skinned one. And how very often he gets his own back on the black Negro: in the Southern States more often than not it is the Jew who is one of the most fanatical upholders of white supremacy. How difficult it is in this tangle of emotions, fears, prejudices, and racial arrogance to find one's identity, and how almost impossible it is to discover a satisfactory understanding of all the complexities of the situation.

Some thirty or thirty-five years ago the Jewish intellectual did not, I think, feel any need to define his role and his identity. To take my own case: I myself would not have discussed such a question as this. Not because I had no roots in the Jewish tradition. On the contrary. I was brought up in a Jewish environment, in a strictly Talmudic school; I wore my sidelocks and my long *kapota* until I was seventeen. Early in life I rebelled against Jewish religious orthodoxy, but I was attracted by the elements of the secular Yiddish culture which manifested itself in literature and the theatre. I myself wrote Yiddish, and in Yiddish I addressed large meetings of workers—not always political meetings. I still see before me the masses of young and old, workers and artisans and paupers, who flocked in the evenings to listen to the readings of poetry and drama. They often came in their working overalls to applaud Peretz Markish or Itzik Manger reciting poems, or Joseph Opatoshu or J. N. Weissenberg reading prose, or H. D. Nomburg reminiscing about Yiddish writers of the past. Nowhere in the world, nowhere in the highly civilized world, except perhaps in Moscow today, were people so thrilled by listening to their writers and poets as were the Jewish workers of Warsaw and of the Polish-Lithuanian provinces. Here something like a new Jewish cultural consciousness was forming itself, and it was doing so through a sharp break with the religious consciousness.

From that time on I spent my best years, my politically active years, among Jewish workers. I was writing in Polish and in Yiddish and I felt that my identity was merged with the labour movement of Eastern Europe in general, and of

Poland in particular. As Marxists we tried theoretically to deny that the Jewish labour movement had an identity of its own, but it had it all the same. It was quite obvious that in that Jewish labour movement the intellectual found his role and did not have to go to the trouble of defining it. From the Jewish working class in Eastern Europe came the efflorescence of Yiddish literature. That language, vigorous, pithy, constantly renewing and enriching itself, was to become, almost overnight, a dead language. Jewish writers and poets were anchored in that labour movement which we saw sinking into nothingness, like an Atlantis.

We all know how repellent are some of the Jewish milieus of the West, the milieus in which there is nothing but a few taboos and a lot of money. With us, in the environment I knew, it was the reverse: no money, no taboos, but an abundance of hope, ideas, and ideals. We had a thorough contempt for the *Yahudim* of the West. Our comrades were made of different stuff.

In the late thirties I had an opportunity to work in close political contact with a man nearly twenty years my senior. Born in utter poverty, he grew up among the worst *Lumpenproletariat* and riff-raff of the city, at the very bottom of the social scale, illiterate till the age of seventeen. When I got to know him he was one of the best educated worker-intellectuals I have ever encountered in any country. Where he learned to read, I never knew. But it was in the prison cells of Tsarist Russian and Piłsudski's Poland, at the Leninist courses in Moscow and discussion circles of revolutionary underground movements that he absorbed eagerly and avidly all that world literature and classical socialist literature had to offer. To this child of the most horrifying Jewish poverty a crumb of knowledge was always far more precious than a chunk of bread. The first Russian revolution of 1905 was a flash of lightning which illumined his horizons; and by its light—in and out of prison—he read the works of Marx, Engels, Kautsky; he read Tolstoy's novels, Mickiewicz's poems, and Peretz's dramas. 'Without the revolution I would have sunk into the swamp of the criminal underworld of Smocha Street', he says of himself in his *Memoirs*. But he left Smocha Street, with its prostitutes and its brothels, its pickpockets and burglars, its moral and physical degradation, far behind him. Truly, he climbed from the Vale of Tears of his childhood to the spiritual heights of the time. He had to know what he was fighting for and he got to know what it was. There was no place for him in the society into which he was born—his life was dedicated to changing it. In the Muranov District of Warsaw he was in the vanguard of the Jewish workers: they all had their identity stamped on their faces, in their eyes, on their toil-worn hands. We, Jewish intellectuals, who were concerned with their lot, with their development and education, with their aspirations and longings, we also had our well-defined identity without ever seeking it.

The *Yahudim* of the West, the bourgeoisie and plutocracy, had to carry their Tales and Tefilim as something that would boost their sense of respectability and dignity. They had to keep up with the gentile Jones', who every Sunday carried their Prayer Book to Church. We had our dignity and we had no need to boost it. We knew the Talmud, we had been steeped in Khassidism. All its idealizations were for us nothing but dust thrown into our eyes. We had grown up in that Jewish past. We had the eleventh, and thirteenth and sixteenth centuries of Jewish history living next door to us and under our very roof; and we wanted to escape it and live in the twentieth century. Through all the thick gilt and varnish of romanticists like Martin Buber, we could see, and smell, the obscurantism of our archaic religion and a way of life unchanged since the middle ages. To someone of my background the fashionable longing of the Western Jew for a return to the sixteenth century, a return which is supposed to help him in recovering, or re-discovering, his Jewish cultural identity, seems unreal and Kafkaesque.

\* \* \*

To switch from personal reminiscence to more general problems: When one raises the question of the Jewish identity, one starts from the assumption of the existence of a positive identity. But are we entitled to make such an assumption? In this period of the history of the world is not Jewish consciousness a reflex, in the main, of anti-semitic pressures? I suppose that if anti-semitism had not proved so terribly deep-rooted, persistent, and powerful in Christian-European civilization, the Jews would not have existed by now as a distinct community—they would have become completely assimilated. What has been permanently re-creating Jewry and imparting ever new vitality to it, has been a hostile gentile environment. Three hundred years ago Spinoza saw nothing miraculous in the fact that the Jews survived their dispersion and loss of state for so long. They have, says Spinoza, 'incurred universal hatred by cutting themselves off completely from all other peoples'.[1] He ascribes their survival largely to the hostility of the gentiles; he recalls that when the King of Spain compelled the Jews either to accept the religion of his realm or to go into exile, a great number of them embraced Roman Catholicism and

[1] *Treatise on Religion and Politics*, Chapt. III.

after doing so were granted all the privileges and honours due to other citizens. Soon they identified themselves with the Spaniards and in a few years' time merged with the local population. The opposite occurred in Portugal. When Manuel I forced the Jews to embrace his religion, they did become 'converted'; but he still did not think them worthy of any position of honour; and so they continued to live apart from the Portuguese community.

One may argue that what arouses such negative emotions must in itself be a positively defined character or identity. Nevertheless, some time ago, say at the turn of the century, this 'positively defined identity' of the Jews was in the process of dissolution. After all, it was in protest against that dissolution that Zionism came into being, whereas European socialism as a rule accepted and encouraged the assimilation of the Jews as part of a wider and progressive movement in consequence of which modern society was supposed to be shedding its particularist and nationalist traditions.

For many centuries the positive element of Jewish identity was rooted in the exceptional role the Jew played in European society; in the age of feudalism and early capitalism he represented the money-economy and its ideas to people whose ways of thinking were conditioned by natural economy. It was not a matter of chance that in the Christian mind the Jew was identified with a symbol like Shylock, or Fagin, a symbol which appears in world literature in many versions and varieties. Nor was it a *meshumad's* malice that caused Marx to say that the Jews' real God was Money. He intended this not as a moral condemnation of Jewry, but as a factual statement about the Jews' particular function in Christian society. He went on to say that Christian society, as it grew more and more capitalist, was becoming more and more 'judaized'. He was firmly convinced that, as European society moved from capitalism to socialism, both the Christian and the Jew would cease to be 'Jewish', or, for that matter, Christian. And in Marx's lifetime, which was the age of assimilation, the Jewish identity was indeed in the process of vanishing, at least in Western Europe.

To my mind the tragic events of the Nazi era neither invalidate the classical Marxist analysis of the Jewish Question nor call for its revision. It goes without saying that classical Marxism made no allowance for anything like the Nazis' 'Final Solution', or for the grave complications of the problem in the Stalinist and post-Stalinist period in the Soviet Union. Classical Marxism reckoned with a healthier and more normal development of our civilization in general, i.e. with a timely transformation of the capitalist into a socialist society. It did not reckon with the persistent survival of capitalism and with its degenerative effects on our civilization at large. Nevertheless, Marx, Engels, Rosa Luxemburg, and Trotsky repeatedly said that mankind was confronted by the alternative of either international socialism or barbarism—*tertium non datur*. Probably they themselves did not know just how right they were and just how real the alternative was. They could not, however, foresee to what depths of barbarism mankind, failing to embrace socialism, would sink.

Nazism was nothing but the self-defence of the old order against communism. The Nazis themselves felt that their role consisted in this; the whole of German society saw them in this role; and European Jewry has paid the price for the survival of capitalism, for the success of capitalism in defending itself against a socialist revolution. This fact surely does not call for a revision of the classical Marxist analysis—it rather confirms it. A doctor, confronted with a particularly vicious type of cancer, certainly would not feel the need or the justification for a revision of medical science. The fate of the Jews does not weaken my Marxist conviction, on the contrary, its supports my Marxist *Weltanschauung*.

Marxism as a method and a materialist conception of history helps in analysing the forces which shape society. Those who have used this method had a premonition—and in the case of Trotsky an extraordinary vision—of the savagery which threatened to engulf Europe. But the full horror, the degeneracy, the pathological character of Nazi theory and practice defied normal and sane human imagination.

It is a tragic and macabre truth that the greatest 're-definer' of the Jewish identity has been Hitler; and this is one of his minor posthumous triumphs. Auschwitz was the terrible cradle of the new Jewish consciousness and of the new Jewish nation. We, who have rejected the religious tradition, now belong to the negative community of those, who have, so many times in history, even so recently and tragically, been singled out for persecution and extermination. For those who have always stressed Jewishness and its continuity, it is strange and bitter to think that the extermination of six million Jews should have given such a new lease of life to Jewry. I would have preferred the six million men, women, and children, to survive and Jewry to perish. It was from the ashes of six million Jews that the phoenix of Jewry has risen. What a resurrection!

And now this new, tragically resurrected, identity is crying out to define itself, to locate itself in the reality shattered by the recent past. This desperate effort will be fruitless if it is made on the basis of an all-Jewish approach.

Who is it who sets out *à la recherche de son identité juive*:
Sir Isaac Wolfson or Mendès-France? Ben Gurion or Lazar
Kaganovich? The Chief Rabbi of Great Britain or myself?

To speak personally once again: to me the Jewish community is still only negative. I have nothing in common
with the Jews of, say, *Mea Shaarim* or with any kind of
Israeli nationalists. I am attracted to the left-wing Marxists
in Israel, but I feel just as close to like-minded people in
France, Italy, Britain, and Japan, or to those masses of
Americans whom I addressed in Washington and San Fran-
cisco at vast protest meetings against the war in Vietnam.
Are we now going to accept the idea that it is racial ties or
'bonds of blood' that make up the Jewish community?
Would not that be another triumph for Hitler and his
degenerate philosophy?

If it is not race, what then makes a Jew?

Religion? I am an atheist. Jewish nationalism? I am an
internationalist. In neither sense am I, therefore, a Jew. I
am, however, a Jew by force of my unconditional solidarity
with the persecuted and exterminated. I am a Jew because
I feel the Jewish tragedy as my own tragedy; because I feel
the pulse of Jewish history; because I should like to do all
I can to assure the real, not spurious, security and self-
respect of the Jews.

The difference in the background, in the conditions of
existence, in the *Weltanschauung*, that separate, say, Sir
Isaac Wolfson or the Chief Rabbi of Great Britain from
myself and my friend from the Muranov district of Warsaw
—whose portrait I sketched on purpose—underline the
incongruity of an all-Jewish approach to the problem which
preoccupies us. The definition of a Jew is so elusive precisely because the Diaspora exposed the Jews to such a

tremendous variety of pressures and influences, and also to such a diversity of means with which they had to defend themselves from hostility and persecution. My own involvement with Jewish affairs in pre-war Poland no doubt would be considered subversive, heretical, and thoroughly un-Jewish to all the congregations of the Synagogues of New York, Paris, and London.

To speak of the 'Jewish community' as if it were an all-embracing entity, then, is meaningless, and for a Marxist doubly so. The Marxist sees all societies primarily from the point of view of their class divisions. But the 'Jewish community' contains not only antagonistic social classes; it has also been divided, so to speak, geographically. The native cultural tradition of each country where the Jews were a minority, affected them differently and left a different imprint on their mental outlook. (Tensions and animosities between the German and East European Jews, for example, still persist and are the subjects of innumerable wry jokes even now in Israel.)

In Eastern Europe secularist Yiddish cultural life was inextricably bound up with the labour movement. That life, that movement, cannot be resuscitated any more. Its splinters in the United States and elsewhere are surely in the process of extinction. One can, of course, cultivate Yiddish as one cultivates any tradition to which nothing more can be added. I remember about forty years ago discussing this question with Moshe Nadir, a great master of Yiddish and a master also of the paradox. At that time people were already discussing the chances of the survival or development of Yiddish in America. Nadir was sceptical: 'I do not believe', he said, 'that Yiddish will survive; but I do not mind if it does not. If our language dies out, we, Yiddish writers, will be read and studied as are the masters of any dead literature —Greek or Latin. We shall become classics. The future generations will read my satires as we now read and study Horace or Ovid.'

Nadir's paradox has come true much earlier and in a much grimmer manner than he could have imagined. In spite of his apparent, or feigned, indifference to the fate of his language, Nadir would have been eager to find means of sharing with English-speaking readers the full flavour of Yiddish poetry and prose and to convey to them the richness of the Yiddish literary heritage. But he was aware that no matter how intelligent, tender, and loving these efforts might be, they would have in them that element of archaeological research, of the work that goes into restoring and presenting fragments of a colossal Pompeii. It is true that thousands or even tens of thousands of Jews still speak Yiddish, but this is too narrow a base for the growth of any live literature or culture.

Remnants of the Jews are scattered all over the world, and some secularist tradition finds expression in other languages. The Jewish element has acquired prominence in the modern American novel. But this cannot in any degree contribute to the survival of the genuine Jewish tradition. A long time ago, and to this day, Jewish writers have debated this question: Is Heine a Jewish writer? Is Boerne? Should they be considered as Jews or simply as Germans? There is not and there cannot be a clearcut answer. Heine wrestled with his Jewish dilemma all his life; so did Boerne. '*Gestern noch ein Held gewesen, ist man heute schon ein Schurke*'— 'Yesterday a hero, today you are a villain only'—Heine commented on Boerne's 'conversion' to Christianity, only to follow soon in his footsteps in order to obtain, through baptism, 'an entrance ticket to European civilization'. A generation later the burden of their Jewishness seemed lighter on such German writers as Franz Werfel, Arnold and Stefan Zweig, Wasserman, and the many others who acquired world fame in the pre-Nazi era.

Quite a few Polish writers have been of Jewish origin, for instance Julian Tuwim and Antoni Słonimski, the most eminent poets of the inter-war period. The Jewish *motif* sometimes appeared in their writings, but only fleetingly, until the massacre of the ghettoes gave a new dimension to their poetry. Even so, they never had the intense consciousness of their Jewishness of, say, Isaac Babel, the Bolshevik who fought in the civil war, and lived, and was drowned, in the sea of the Russian revolution.

In Russia the Pale of Settlement made any organic spiritual growing together of Jews and Slavs impossible. In Poland Jews lived in virtual ghettoes even before 1940. Polish nationalism, anti-semitism, and Catholic clericalism on the one hand, and Jewish separatism, orthodoxy, and Zionism on the other, worked against a lasting and fruitful symbiosis. It was, we should remember, the theorists of Zionism and not only those of socialism, who spoke of the unproductive character of the Jewish 'economy' in the Diaspora; an antagonism between the productive and unproductive elements of society was inevitable in any case; and upon this socially and economically determined antagonism there grew over the centuries the huge superstructure of ideological estrangement. Such was the estrangement that in Poland, for instance, there never existed any point of contact between Polish and Yiddish literature. To put it more accurately, Polish writers, academicians, educationists were not even aware of the fact that Warsaw was the centre of a flourishing modern Yiddish literature, read and admired by Jews (and not only Jews) all over the world.

At the turn of the century the situation in Russia was more complicated. Russian culture had an immense power of assimilation, largely because of the universal character of the ideas which have animated it in the modern age, the ideas of Tolstoy, Plekhanov, Lenin. It is difficult, however, to speak of any specifically Jewish influence on Russian culture. Incidentally, Jews did not even begin to enter Russian literature before the 1890s; and they entered it for good only with the revolution—this was their 'entrance ticket' to the culture that for centuries kept them at a distance. Isaac Babel had hardly any predecessors, and the Jew who was the greatest master of Russian prose in the generation of the revolution was Leon Trotsky, yet it was not *qua* Jew that he exercised an influence. Jewish themes entered Polish literature much earlier, and the Jewish problem intensely occupied Polish poets and novelists before Poland had regained her independence, from Mickiewicz to Orzeszkowa and Konopnicka. Yet, I fear, the Jewish *motifs* in their poems and novels sound quite exotic and esoteric—perhaps even completely unintelligible—to the new generation of Poles growing up in Poland without Jews.

Is it at all possible that no trace should be left of the Jewish presence in Eastern Europe? Some traces are certainly left; but whether in the long run they will have more meaning than the traces that the Red Indians have left on the American civilization of today is another matter. For Jews of our generation it is extremely difficult to absorb the reality of Central and Eastern Europe being *judenrein*, i.e.

of the elimination of the whole social element which once had its tremendous weight.

In Israel today there is, so to speak, a new mutation of the Jew and his identity. Israel's cultural consciousness is Hebrew, and, drawing historical nourishment from the Bible and the Talmud and medieval liturgy, it is sustained by the ghosts of the past. The *Mea Shaarim* has not produced any literature at all, because to the truly orthodox Jew any secular writing in Hebrew is almost blasphemy. No matter how the young modern writer may emphasize his break with the religious tradition and his independence from it, he has to dig into the past in order to revive the language which was, like Latin, dead for nearly two millennia. It survived in theology and now cannot easily achieve secularization. Tradition has its objective logic and is bound to weigh heavily on the new generation of Israeli men of letters. As for myself, I cannot accept this new Hebrew mutation of the Jewish consciousness and absorb it into my identity. For that I have been too strongly formed by an international European tradition, Polish and Russian, German and English, and above all, Marxist. Hebrew belonged to my childhood and early adolescence. Having broken with it and rejected it then, I cannot go back to it now.

\* \* \*

An unrepentant Marxist, an atheist, an internationalist— in what sense am I then a Jew? What is it that brings me near that 'negative community'?

Paradoxically, I come unexpectedly close to the fears of an orthodox Jew and a Zionist. I do not believe that antisemitism is a spent force. I fear that we may be living in a fools' paradise in our Western welfare state. The trustful feeling of freedom from anti-semitism may well be one more illusion, a particularly Jewish one, engendered by our 'affluent society'.

Trotsky, confronted with the phenomenon of Nazism, described it as 'the collected refuse of international political thought' which went into the making of the 'intellectual treasure of the new Germanic Messianism'. It stirred and rallied all the forces of barbarism lurking under the thin surface of 'civilized' class society. In a memorable phrase, alive with the premonition of gas chambers, Trotsky thus summed up the essence of Nazism: 'Everything which society, if it had developed normally [i.e. towards socialism], would have rejected . . . as the excrement of culture, is now bursting out through its throat: capitalist civilization is disgorging undigested barbarity . . .'. I do not believe that our bourgeois society in the West (and this unfortunately goes also for the post-capitalist society in Russia) has been able to digest and get out of its system that barbarity of ages which Hitler represented. I have heard it recalled how, when the era of rationalism began, Jews assumed universal tolera-tion and said to each other: 'Let us not bother any more about the Talmud and the Torah—let us all dance around the goddess of reason.' That goddess of reason was the goddess that failed. She was a highly bourgeois goddess, the patron of a society whose preoccupation with money-making (not an exclusively Jewish preoccupation!) did not allow it to digest barbarism. This is a society which at every moment of acute insecurity whips up racialism, nationalism, xeno-phobia, the hatred and the fear of the alien. And who is as alien as the Jew?

Let us not imagine now that in this Indian summer of post-war bourgeois prosperity we are dancing again around the goddess of reason and that this time she is not going to fail us, but will bestow on us all her favours for good and all. Even in this mild, highly liberal and highly civilized English society we see swastikas cropping up here and there, scribbled on the blocks of flats in 'respectable' districts. From my own experience I know that looking for a flat in London, in Hampstead, say, you can be told that the neighbours would object to a Negro tenant or a Jew moving in, but they would certainly welcome *you* as an 'exception'. Yes, under the smooth surface the barbarity is there, rough and raw, always ready to surge up.

We may have the impression that anti-semitism is a spent force because in this our welfare state people are, on the whole, contented and satisfied and their social troubles are seemingly dispelled. Let this society suffer any severe shock, such as it is bound to suffer; let there be again millions of unemployed, and we will see the same lower middle class alliance with the *Lumpenproletariat*, from whom Hitler recruited his following, running amok with anti-semitism. As long as nation-state imposes its supremacy and as long as we have not an international society in existence, as long as the wealth of every nation is in the hands of one national capitalist oligarchy, we shall have chauvinism, racialism, and, as its culmination, anti-semitism. That is why I think that the role of the intellectuals—Jews and non-Jews alike—of those who are aware of the depth of the Jewish tragedy and of the menace of its recurrence, is to remain eternal protesters: to maintain the opposition to the powers that be, to militate against the taboos and conventions, to struggle for a society in which nationalism and racialism will at last lose their hold on the human mind. I know that this is no easy way out; it may be distressing and hurtful; and for those who take it there can be no precise formulation of a set of precepts for action. But if we do not remain pro-testers, we shall be moving within a vicious and pernicious circle, a suicidal circle.

When one looks at the record of the Jewish intellectuals in the West, one comes to rather sad and disappointing conclusions. What is so striking about the Jewish intellec-tuals in the West is precisely their extraordinary conformism, political, ideological, and social. In the cold war which has dominated our lives for more than thirteen years, the Jews have been most prominent. From this indictment I would exclude perhaps those engaged in purely scientific studies. But when we move to the departments of humanities we see among the hosts of historians, politicians, sociologists, etc., a great number of Jews furiously engaged in this cold war on behalf of this society of ours with its undigested barbarity. When one looks at the legions of Panglosses who proclaim that 'our American way of life' or 'our British way of life' is the best possible of all ways of life, one is sometimes tempted to pray that some *numerus clausus* should be im-posed on the access of the Jewish intellectuals to the Pangloss profession in which they are so vocal and in such relative majority. Far be it from me to react to them in assuming the role of Cassandra, for I still trust that the 'eternal pro-testant' (I am allowing myself to use Professor Daiches ex-pression) will see his ideals achieved and his hopes fulfilled. Only if the search for an identity can help the Jewish in-tellectual in his struggle for a better future for the whole of mankind, is that search at all, in my view, justified.

# III

# The Russian Revolution and the
# Jewish Problem[1]

ANYONE approaching the topic of this lecture, the Russian Revolution and the Jewish problem, must do so with trepidation, because it is an extremely complex and many-sided question. Nothing would be easier, and more harmful, than to simplify it, to try and apportion blame—to blame the Jews, or the revolution, or the Russians. We must also beware of thinking of this problem in the familiar terms of the relationship between revolutionary Russia and other nationalities of the Soviet Union. In this sense the 'Jewish problem' is unique. To see it in all its true complexity we should go back to its origin. We should analyse briefly the structure of the Jewish population at the beginning of the revolution, investigate the place of the Jews in Russian society, follow the changes and metamorphoses of the Russian revolution itself, and appraise the impact of all these changes on the fate of the Jews in the Soviet Union. The main question we have to face and answer candidly is this: Why has the Russian revolution not succeeded, in the course of nearly half a century, in solving the Jewish problem?

[1] The text of a lecture given to the Jewish Society of the London School of Economics Students' Union on 29 October 1964.

I must begin by drawing a sharp contrast between the place of Jews in Western societies and their place in Eastern Europe and especially in Russia; and by warning that to look at the Jewish problem in Russia through the prism of Jewish life in Western Europe, is to see with distorted vision and embark on an inquiry that will lead you nowhere. You must not for a single moment imagine that Jewish life and the Jewish community in Eastern Europe and in Russia resembled in any way the Jewish community in England, in France, or even in the United States.

Throughout the nineteenth century the Jews in the countries of Western Europe belonged mainly to the middle class. There were very few Jewish workers, not many Jewish artisans, some small shopkeepers. Most Jews were merchants, transacting their business on a large scale in many western capitals. Some of them were great bankers, and the House of Rothschild became almost a symbol of the Jewish *haute bourgeoisie*. This predominantly bourgeois character of the Jewish community in Western Europe stood in marked contrast to the Jewish communities in Eastern Europe. True, in the East we also possessed our Jewish bourgeoisie, our merchants or shopkeepers. But the great majority of Jews were poor toilers, primitive artisans, cobblers, tailors, carpenters, and what were grandly called 'metal workers'. But make no mistake and do not think in terms of, say, French *metallos* or British steel workers. Those 'metal workers', as I knew them, were mostly plumbers, tinkers, locksmiths. They used to form some sort of fraternity and call it the Trade Union of Metal Workers. It was a colossal boost to all those paupers to belong to a union with such a grandiose name; but they were paupers all the the same. Imagine a population of millions of destitute, poverty-stricken Jews, among them a host of so-called *Luftmenschen*, that is people without any roots in the social structure of society, without any occupation, without any regular livelihood; hawkers, rag and bone men, people who made a living as match-makers—they did not make matches but marriages and weddings, and haggled over the percentage of the dowry that was to be their reward.

In Western Europe after the French revolution the Jews enjoyed formal equality in the eyes of the law. (In 1847 Lionel Rothschild, the first Jewish M.P., was elected to the House of Commons.) This equality before the law went hand in hand with the growing assimilation of the Jewish community, for even those sections which preserved their religion and Jewish consciousness became assimilated through adopting the language of the countries they lived in and acquiring the outward appearance of their compatriots. In Eastern Europe the great masses of Jews, millions of them, lived in compact communities, separated from their non-Jewish environment. These ghettoes were not formal; Jews were allowed to go out of them and they did indeed go out. Nevertheless they lived in close communities, wore distinct clothes—complete with beards and sidelocks, spoke their own language, developed their own culture, their own literature; their knowledge of Polish or Russian was often less than rudimentary. Their tongue remained Yiddish. There was also, of course, a minority of educated Jews who became more and more assimilated and indistinguishable in their habits and customs from the indigenous intelligentsia. But the way of life of the great mass of orthodox Jews had developed very little in the course of centuries. They still carried on a kind of primitive trade such as had been practised in the sixteenth or seventeenth centuries; and their religious taboos and rites were equally archaic and anachronistic.

In Western Europe along with the assimilation went the emancipation of the Jews. Not so in Eastern Europe. In Russia, in particular, the Jews had the status of 'citizens of the second or third category'. They were not allowed to settle in Russia proper but only within the so-called Jewish pale; they were not allowed to own land; certain occupations were closed to them. Their position was little better than that of the Russian and Polish peasant serfs. But peasants were at least not subjected to the pogroms, outbursts of anti-semitism and wholesale massacres, which were both spontaneous and yet very often encouraged by the authorities. It is a significant fact that the word 'pogrom' is of Russian origin, though by now it has entered most European languages. Only five years before the Russian revolution there was the famous Bayliss trial in Kiev which epitomized the position of the Jews under the Tsar. In this trial—the so-called ritual murder trial—a Jew, Bayliss, was accused of having killed a gentile child in order to use its blood for the *matzos* at Pesach (Easter). On the rampage were the Black Hundreds, the societies of vicious and fierce reactionaries or Greek Orthodox obscurantists fostered by Tsardom. Here you have the extraordinary contrast between the uncertain existence of the Jew in Russia and Jewish life in the West. You may say that in the West too we had an eruption of anti-semitism—the Dreyfus affair—but this was on a very different level of social and political development. Nevertheless, there is no doubt that the Dreyfus affair marked a turning point in the history of Jews in Western Europe. It was towards the end of the nineteenth century that the progressive movement of emancipation suffered a tremendous setback and anti-semitism began to show itself, to grow, and finally to reach the macabre proportions of the Nazi era. The century after the French revolution brought enlightenment and progress, and with them the assimilation of the Jews with their environment. But in Eastern Europe it was a century of oppression and isolation for the Jews.

Such was the situation of the Jews when late in the 1890s and early 1900s the Social Democratic movement began to spread and to acquire its mass character. It is now very often said that the attitude to the Jews, as we observe it in Russia today, corresponds to that worked out originally by Lenin and the Bolsheviks. It is fashionable, especially among the Jews, to blame Bolshevism and communism for all the misfortunes that have befallen their co-religionists in Russia. Yet when we go back to the original sources, when we scrutinize the documents, we find that up to the revolution the Bolsheviks and the Mensheviks, and even the Social Revolutionaries—absolutely all currents of Russian socialism—were agreed on the approach to the Jewish problem. In this the Russian Bolshevik Lenin and the Menshevik Jew Martov or the Jew Trotsky were of one mind. They took over their ideas about the Jews from Western Marxists and from Marx and Engels in particular. In one of his famous essays on the Jewish problem, written in the 1840s, Marx said that the question of the emancipation of the Jews no longer existed as an independent issue: all endeavours should be directed towards the emancipation of European society, especially Western society, from capitalism. Once the heavy yoke of capitalist oppression was thrown off, all members of society, including the Jews, would achieve equality and freedom.

In early Marxist writings on this subject there was even an undercurrent of a certain hostility towards the Jews, not as Jews, but as a prominent and spectacular section of Western European bourgeoisie. The Rothschilds symbolized the power, the financial domination of the Jewish bourgeoisie among the French, the British, and the German middle classes. On the other hand, there were the eminent leaders of socialism of Jewish origin such as Marx and Lassalle. But again, towards the end of the nineteenth century, as anti-semitism began to grow even in Western society, the whole socialist movement became seriously preoccupied with the Jewish problem; it was then that August Bebel, the great leader of the German Social Democracy, wrote his famous work on anti-semitism calling it 'the socialism of the fools'. This was more than a brilliant paradox or a witty epigram. The fact was that the conspicuous role of the Jews among the bankers and the merchants did arouse antagonism towards the Jews among the poorer classes of western society. Bebel and the other socialists, among them Kautsky, tried to explain to the workers that they should direct their fight not just against the Jewish bourgeoisie which was, after all, only a small section of the capitalist class, but against the bourgeoisie as a whole. This was real socialism; only fools sought to change the social system by turning against some members—the Jewish members—of the oppressing class. In retrospect we can see how farsighted were Bebel and his comrades, when they pointed out that the capitalists of Western Europe were ready to sacrifice their Jewish brothers as scapegoats and were even prepared to incite workers, the *Lumpenproletariat*, and the petty shopkeepers against the Jewish bourgeoisie to save their own life and property. This would be the cheapest way of turning away from themselves the pent-up hatred of the oppressed masses.

In Western Europe there were no Jewish workers, or only very few, and consequently there was no Jewish working class movement. The socialist leaders stuck to the view that the only answer to the Jewish question was total assimilation. At that time Lenin as well as all his comrades were proudly proclaiming themselves to be pupils of German Social Democracy and so they too believed that in Russia the problem would also be solved by assimilation, by a total absorption of Jewish communities in the great socialist society. They very soon saw, however, that in the East the problem was much tougher than in the West, precisely because the Jewish paupers, workers, and the lower middle classes lived in isolated areas, in compact ghettoes, cultivating and perpetuating their own mode of life. In spite of this, Lenin and Martov, Bolsheviks and Mensheviks, were absolutely determined to draw the Jewish workers into the struggle of their Russian comrades against Tsardom and against the old order that ruled in Eastern Europe. The same view was held by that great woman revolutionary of Jewish origin, Rosa Luxemburg, who was even more bent on the assimilation of the Jews than either Lenin or Martov.

At this period Zionism too began to develop as a political movement, drawing its support mainly from the Jewish communities in Western countries. It should be realized that the great majority of Eastern European Jews were, up to the outbreak of the second World War, opposed to Zionism. This is a fact of which most Jews and non-Jews in the West are seldom aware. The Zionists in our part of the world were a significant minority, but they never succeeded in attracting a majority of their co-religionists. The most fanatical enemies of Zionism were precisely the workers, those who spoke Yiddish, those who considered themselves Jews; they were the most determined opponents of the idea of an emigration from Eastern Europe to Palestine. In Poland, in 1939, the Jewish population was for the last time electing the leaders of its communities, the *Kehilahs*. The communists, who were then very influential, regarded the *Kehilahs* as clerical institutions and boycotted the elections. The fiercely anti-Zionist *Bund* (Jewish Workers Party) took part and polled the great majority of the votes. (Only a relatively small sector of the socialist movement, the *Poaley Zion*, tried to combine socialism with Zionism.) Jewish opinion in the West very often equates anti-Zionism with anti-semitism. According to this view the Jews of Eastern Europe in their great majority, were just anti-semites. But this conclusion, of course, is an absurdity.

This Jewish opposition to Zionism was a tragic opposition—it failed and ended in the perdition of the Jews. In the idea of an evacuation, of an exodus from the countries in which they had their homes and in which their ancestors had lived for centuries, the anti-Zionists saw an abdication of their rights, a yielding to hostile pressure, a surrender to anti-semitism. To them anti-semitism seemed to triumph in Zionism, which recognized the legitimacy and the validity of the old cry: 'Jews, get out!' The Zionists were agreeing to 'get out'.

Among the Jews of Eastern Europe the feeling that only the overthrow of Tsardom by way of revolution could relieve the discrimination and oppression to which they were subjected, became almost universal; and Jews played a very prominent part in the revolutionary movement.

But when the revolution did come, the sudden transformation of society had also a painful and disintegrating impact on a considerable segment of the Jewish population. Since so many Jews in Russia were petty shopkeepers, artisans, speculators, and *Luftmenschen*, the revolution of necessity sought to re-make the whole structure of their lives. What the socialists wanted to achieve was the so-called productivization of the Jews, their conversion into factory workers, into farmers, into a modern labour force. The shopkeeper found himself on the brink of an abyss: the new order did not favour him. True, it freed him from the fear of pogroms and persecution, but it threatened his accustomed way of life as a middle man and as a primitive trader. In the 1920s the Bolsheviks began to encourage the Jews to settle on the land, in Jewish colonies in the Crimea, in Kherson, in Birobidjan. At the time I visited these colonies and I witnessed the extraordinary efforts that some idealistic '*goyim*' and some enthusiastic Jews were making to transform at least a section of the Jewish population into good farmers. Considerable investments and tremendous exertions went into this task of changing the mentality of the *Luftmensch*. He was expected to discard the art and the tricks of petty commerce and to be slowly taught the art of ploughing and hoeing the soil. But all these efforts to turn the trader into a farmer failed. The Jews were simply not prepared for such a break, for such a deep and profound change in their whole mode of existence. Even in Israel today only a very small minority of the population lives on the land, in the kibbutzim; the great majority of Jews still rush to the town and prefer to be an urban population than to be country folk and peasants.[1] No wonder. For centuries the Jews had been city dwellers,

---

[1] In Israel, in 1965, over two million Jews lived in towns and only 267,000 on the land.

and the urban tradition has become second nature to them. Only the most idealistic Zionists, those who wanted to settle on the sacred soil of Zion, emigrated from Russia and took to the plough. Those who remained in the Soviet Union had no inclination to become farmers. They had to enter modern industry. Very many of them did become workers in large-scale factories, but these were still a minority. The great majority, with their urban tradition and a level of education higher, on the whole, than that of the Russian population, became white-collar workers, and entered *en masse* into the ranks of the post-revolutionary bureaucracy, into the party and state offices and institutions. They also played a great role in the academic world—even today, for all the outcry, often justified, about anti-semitic discrimination, there are well over 25,000 Jews as academic teachers in the U.S.S.R. This process of wholesale higher education began, of course, only after 1917, when the *numerus clausus* was abolished and the doors of Russian Universities were thrown open to Jewish students.

Despite all this, even in the most heroic period of the revolution there was an undercurrent of the old persistent anti-semitism among the Russian population. Where should we look for the source of this accursed poison? First of all in the backwardness, the benightedness, and the illiteracy of the masses of Russian *muzhiks*, and even of some sections of the urban workers as well. There was the fatal influence of the Greek Orthodox Church, the most obscurantist of all the Churches in Europe. There was the deeply ingrained Christian myth about the Jews as the crucifiers of Christ; that myth which, we now realize, has permeated the mind of the whole Christian civilization much more thoroughly than people had imagined even fifty years ago. (At the threshold of the scientific twentieth century there was the hope that our modern age was emancipating itself, shedding the religious prejudices and the baneful influence of myths and legends!) As elsewhere, so in Russia, the prejudice and hatred that had been inculcated into the minds of people over centuries and millennia, were not to be rooted out in the course of a few years or even decades. This was not all. Another ingredient fed the anti-semitism of the masses. The poor Russian peasant looked with distrust at the Jewish village shopkeeper or innkeeper, whose trade was often fraudulent. In that abysmal misery in which the latter lived, he may have tried to relieve his own poverty at the expense of the *muzhik*, who was as wretched as himself. And here is to be seen the making of that antagonism of the poor peasant or worker towards his Jewish neighbour.

On a different level, Jewish intellectuals or white-collar workers who occupied higher positions in party and state, in army and civilian institutions, in the educational system, and those prominent in the press, the cinema and the theatre, evoked a certain envy and *jalousie de métier*. In Trotsky's correspondence with Lenin during the civil war there is a striking illustration of this atmosphere. Trotsky, then the head of the Red Army and the Commissar of Defence, wrote a confidential message from the front in which he demanded that all Jews in the safe administrative military jobs be withdrawn from their offices and sent to the fronts. There is too much talk among the soldiers, wrote the Jew Trotsky, that more Jews are to be found in remote and secure places than in the front line of the battle. Even during the civil war, when the Red Army was defending the Jews against the pogroms of the White Guards, there was this fatal, but human and understandable tension in the attitude of an ordinary Russian towards the more or less 'privileged' Jew.

In the Lenin era the Bolsheviks conducted a very intense anti-nationalistic, anti-religious, and anti-clerical propaganda. They conducted it with complete impartiality, condemning, denouncing, and trying to eradicate any kind of nationalism, but in the first instance Great Russian chauvinism, and proclaiming the equality of all small nations and national minorities. The Jews were allowed, and even encouraged, to publish their newspapers and their literature in Yiddish, and to develop their theatre—and the Yiddish theatre was one of the best I have known. It is now probably forgotten that the first great Hebrew theatre in history, the *Habima*, was founded in Russia on the initiative of the Commissar of Education, A. V. Lunacharsky. (Incidentally, the *Habima* soon left Russia for Palestine.) There was certainly an inconsistency here: the Bolsheviks were, on principle, opposed to the resuscitation of Hebrew, then a dead language; and when *Habima* performed the *Dybbuk*, Ansky's mystical play, protests were heard against the idealization of the Khassidic religious legends on the stage of Red Russia. But the power of artistic creation was untameable in that brief but stormy golden age of post-revolutionary art.

\*      \*      \*

Clearly, the Bolsheviks took an over-optimistic view of the chances of solving the Jewish problem. They were not alone in underrating the depth of the anti-semitic instinct in Christian folklore. They thought of their revolution as the prelude to a continent-wide upheaval; they imagined that all the progressive forces of Germany and France would help them to move forward; that the sickness of anti-semitism would disappear in a rationally organized, healthy socialist Europe. This was not to be. The Russian revolution remained isolated; the German one was defeated. Europe did not come to the rescue. Russia was left alone to stew in her own juice of backwardness inherited from Tsardom, from centuries of Greek Orthodoxy, illiteracy, poverty, and barbarism. In these conditions all existing antagonisms in Russian society became accentuated, and among them the antagonism between the Jew and the non-Jew. One should not imagine that the Jewish problem existed, so to speak, in a vacuum, that it was independent of what was going on in Soviet society. It was embedded in the structure of that society and closely tied to its development and evolution, to its growth and progress, to retrogression and new progress.

Precisely because the problem we are analyzing forms an organic part of the whole Soviet scene, there is no simple way of going into its every aspect in one or even several lectures. I shall therefore now make a certain logical jump and try to show how the development of the single party system affected the fate of the Jews.

In the Lenin era the monolithic party was unthinkable. But the single party system was already ominously casting its shadow ahead. Up to 1924, and even for the next two or three years, there was still free and open debate among the Bolsheviks and the suppression of other parties was only gradual. To give one example: The Left *Poaley Zion*, the Socialist Zionist Party, existed legally in Russia up to 1925 or 1926. Although the Bolsheviks were opposed to Zionism, the complete suppression of Zionist opinion was not in their programme. I have discussed, in my books on Stalin and Trotsky, the process which resulted in the gradual disappearance of all political parties. Here I can only add that this process automatically, and logically, led to the establishment of the single party system among the Jews too. All Jewish parties—the *Bund*, the *Poaley Zion*, and other Zionist groupings were suppressed. To some extent, and with a great deal of justification, Zionism might have been considered as an ideology alien, or at least unfavourable, to the revolution: it placed all its hopes not on socialism and international solidarity, but on the formation of a separate Jewish state; it aimed not at the creation of a better future for all Soviet peoples in the U.S.S.R., but at the exodus of an organized group from the U.S.S.R. In a word, Zionism turned its back on the revolution, or at best, sought to ignore it. For all this there was no objective reason why Zionism should have been declared a dangerous and subversive doctrine. The argument that 'Zionism threatened the Russian revolution' was spurious and ridiculous in view of the utter impotence of all Jewish groupings in Russia. The fact was that in the monolithic totalitarian regime there was no room for any heterodoxy, for any plurality of views or political currents. (As the old Jewish saying goes: '*Wie es Christelt sich, asoy yidelt sich*' which means: as things go among the Christians, so they also have to go among the Jews.) Since only one party, one outlook, was allowed among the gentiles, only one monolithic outlook could be tolerated among the Jews. Incidentally, the most fanatical advocates of the suppression of Jewish parties were by no means the Russians; they were the Jews themselves, the Jewish communists, the *Yevsektsia* (Jewish Section of the Communist Party). I was in Russia at the time when these problems were hotly debated and I witnessed repeatedly how Russian Bolsheviks, among others Mikhail Kalinin, the President of the U.S.S.R., argued with the Jewish comrades trying to temper their fierce hostility towards the Zionist idea, towards the remnants of the *Bund* and even towards Jewish clericalism. But the Jewish communists felt that they had to be more orthodox, more 'kosher', and more determined than their Russian colleagues. We are usually more intolerant of those with whom we disagree in our own environment, than with opponents who are more remote from us. By the same token we may recall that it was the Georgian Djugashvili and his countrymen who showed the greatest zeal and passion in persecuting 'local nationalism' in Tiflis.

With the single party system came the development and crystallization of Stalinism. The years of isolation, the frustrated hopes of help from outside, the defeat of communism in Europe—all this prepared the ground on which Stalin's doctrine of socialism in one country could take root. To Russia's isolation the Bolsheviks reacted with an ideology of isolation. They made a virtue out of necessity: being cut off from the world, they boycotted the world.

We now know how much of its internationalist tradition the Bolshevik party was made to jettison on the road to socialism in one country on which Stalin was setting out. In Russia, as in the West, anti-semitism invariably worms its way to the surface in times of reaction and feeds and grows on nationalist emotions and hatreds. Stalin, never fastidious in the choice of means, did not shrink from exploiting anti-Jewish tendencies in his struggles with the Opposition. At first surreptitiously, by dark hints and allusions, Stalinist agitators stirred up anti-semitic prejudice, brought it nearer the surface, until in the period of the Great Purges it reached its first climax. The anti-semitic undertones in the propaganda seemed such an enormity then that Trotsky, usually reticent on the subject, could hardly contain himself and wrote in a letter to Bukharin, in March 1926: '... is it true, is it possible that in *our party*, in Moscow, in WORKERS' CELLS, anti-semitic agitation should be carried on with impunity?' To the same indignant question asked at the Politbureau meeting a fortnight later he received no answer—there was some embarrassment and some shrugging of shoulders. It was true that among the leaders of the Opposition Jews were extremely prominent. And Stalin's faithful servants portrayed them as 'rootless cosmopolitans', as people who, not being native sons of Mother Russia, naturally did not care for socialism in one country, in their own Fatherland. This hypocrisy was such that the word Jew was never uttered, but the point in those denunciations of 'rootless cosmopolitans' was well taken.

On the other hand there were many Jews among the Stalinist bureaucracy too. At the head of the forcible collectivization in the Ukraine, where it was carried out in the most cruel and bloody way, stood the Jew Kaganovich. And here you have the tragic impasse in which the Jews were trapped. In town they were persecuted as 'rootless cosmopolitans' opposed to the progress of socialism in Russia; in the countryside they were hated by the peasants who saw in the Bolshevik Jew Kaganovich their chief tormentor. To these contradictions some others, no less thorny, were added. The petty trader, the speculator, the Jewish *Luftmensch* still floated about on the waves of the tremendous upheavals; and he was still arousing the distrust and utter dislike of the Russian population. On the other hand, there were the Jews in the universities, the professors, teachers, the great doctors, who were educating *en masse* a new generation of the intelligentsia and who were contributing so much to the development and modernization of Russia.

All this illustrates how the contradictions inherent in the changing Soviet society tended to affect the Jews more sharply and more cruelly than they could possibly affect any other racial or national group in the U.S.S.R.

Then came the second World War. Of course, during the period of the short-lived conciliation and pact between Hitler and Stalin the Jews in Russia were caught in a cross-fire. Their position became very uncomfortable, to say the least. It was symbolized in the resignation of the Foreign Minister, Maxim Litvinov, and his replacement by the Great Russian Vyacheslav Molotov. How could the Jew Litvinov sign a pact with Hitler or Ribbentrop? For this job a 'pure' Aryan was needed. Something like racial contamination was blowing over from Germany to Russia. These were the days when Stalin and Molotov sent Hitler their message about the Russo-German friendship 'cemented by blood' and when Stalin proclaimed that he was liberating his 'blood brethren' —the Ukrainians—from Polish oppression. Racialist terminology of this kind increasingly 'enriched' Stalinist idiom. This was soon replaced by an intensely nationalistic, chauvinistic Great Russian language. Then came 21 June 1941 and the champion of anti-semitism became the implacable enemy of Soviet Russia again.

After all the upheavals that Russia had undergone in the years just before the war, after the brutalities of forcible collectivization, after the drama of the Great Purges, the deportations of immense masses to concentration camps, after all this, tensions in Soviet society were so acute and dangerous that at the beginning of the war the whole structure—moral, economic, political—seemed on the brink of collapse. In the Ukraine the population at first received Hitler and his occupation armies with relief and even joy.

And this lasted up to the moment when the Nazis showed the Ukrainians what they were really capable of. Very, very soon the Ukrainians came to the bitter conclusion that even at his worst Stalin was still preferable to Hitler. Nevertheless the Nazi invasion of the Ukraine and Western Russia brought with it a new and very powerful wave of anti-semitism. The age-old prejudice, always smouldering, sometimes damped down, but never extinguished, burst out; and the Nazis fanned it into a terrible flame. Stalin and his government on their part were afraid that the war against the Nazis might be seen by the Ukrainians and the Russians as a war fought just in defence of the Jews. The shrill voice of Nazi propaganda, Nazi radio, Nazi leaflets and pamphlets were relentlessly proclaiming to the population of the Soviet Union: 'This war is a Jewish intrigue! You are fighting the war in the interest of the Jews!' And this perverse argument very often seemed plausible to great numbers of Ukrainians and Russians.

Stalin was anxious to counteract this propaganda; and he set about doing it in his own sly and devious way. Instead of attacking it openly and showing its sordid demagogy, he sneakingly tried to trick the whole gruesome theme out of existence. You had, therefore, that very curious phenomenon that throughout the second World War the Soviet press hardly ever reported on the fate of the Jews under the Nazis, hardly ever mentioned Auschwitz and Majdanek. Only rarely and in a manner as casual and as brief as possible were the broad masses of the belligerent U.S.S.R. given scraps of information about the extermination of the Jews. By nature distrustful and contemptuous of his people, Stalin was less than ever inclined to rate their morale highly. In the months of defeat, his propaganda was clumsily manipulated and sounded false. The resulting confusion had sometimes for the Jews tragic consequences which could have been avoided. To give you one example: Taganrog, an expanding industrial city in the area of the Azov Sea, had a large Jewish population. When, in 1942, the Soviet government offered to evacuate the Taganrog Jews before the advancing Nazi armies, they refused to move: they did not believe that the German nation, the nation of Goethe and Beethoven, the nation of poets and thinkers, the nation of . . . Marx and Engels could possibly be guilty of such enormities towards the Jews as the Soviet authorities were now telling them it was. The Jews disbelieved Stalin's propaganda even when that propaganda was true; and they all perished under the German occupation. Those who were evacuated from other places survived.

Despite all of Stalin's crimes we must remember that it was on his orders that two and a half million Jews from the invaded territories of Russia were helped to move towards the interior of the country and thus were saved from Nazi concentration camps and gas chambers. This is a fact which the Jewish nationalist and Zionist press all too often tends to forget. These Jews found themselves in a strange situation: evacuated hurriedly to Kazakhstan, to Uzbekistan, to the central Asian republics, bewildered and despairing, thrown into unfamiliar surroundings, they were again uprooted. They had to make a living amid the tremendous poverty and shortage of food, amid real starvation and hunger, and they became again conspicuous on the black markets, they became again the *Luftmenschen*. (This sad tale was related to me by many of my Polish friends deported to these regions of Russia.) It would be unjust to blame these Jewish evacuees. They were neither farmers nor peasants who could coax something out of the land even in the worst conditions; they were not, most of them, skilled industrial workers—most of them were too old to be drafted into the army. They still had in them something of the mentality of the trader—now heightened by the sense of utter insecurity—who hoards a little tea and sugar, a few sacks of grain and potatoes and sells them at the best price he can get. All around them the mass of the Russian workers were starving. This again gave another impetus to the anti-semitic wave. Nevertheless, these two and a half or three million Jews, the great bulk of the Jewish communities in Russia, were saved from the Nazi massacre.

In the aftermath of the war the nerves of the nation were again on edge. To the chaos and weariness and exhaustion another disaster was added in the year 1946: a catastrophic failure of the harvest such as Russia had not experienced for over half a century. Famine was widespread: and so was despair when the people started counting their dead: they had lost twenty million men in the fighting! The awareness of this tremendous loss came slowly at first. But soon it hit the nation with an unbearable force. One could not see a man on the Russian fields and farms; only women, old men, and children were tilling the land and producing the meagre crops which could hardly feed the nation. All restrictions on the employment of juvenile labour were lifted. Work and over-work was the order of the day.

Old and new antagonisms were sharp and painful. And again there started the almost subterranean struggle between the two great currents in the Russian way of thinking and in the ideology of Soviet society, the struggle between nationalism and internationalism. If one does not bear constantly in mind the fact that this struggle constitutes the basic phenomenon in Soviet society, one misses the key to the understanding of the history of the Stalin period, of the events which followed it, and of the place which the Jewish problem occupies in Soviet life. You have nationalists and anti-semites among the peasants, the workers, the bureaucracy, the intelligentsia. You have internationalists and therefore enemies of anti-semitism in all these layers of society as well.

*          *          *

We should now briefly turn our attention to an act of Stalin's foreign policy which may seem to contradict not only his own attitude towards the Jews, but also the whole traditional Bolshevik view of Zionism.

In 1948, when Israel was forming itself into a State we witnessed a curious situation in which the Russians and the Americans—the two super-antagonists—joined hands. Together they managed to dislodge the British from the Middle East; and together they acted as midwives in the act of birth of Israel.

Whatever Stalin's calculations, it was to him that Israel, paradoxically, was indebted for its independent existence. And it was from Stalinized Czechoslovakia, from the Czech arms factories, that the main arsenal of the *Haganah* came. With these 'tainted' weapons the Jews in Palestine defeated the British and the Arabs. The assistance and the effective material help which Stalin was giving to the Jews seemed to the Western statesmen sinister, aroused resentment, and stirred a not inconsiderable amount of ill-feeling towards the Jews.

Then came the cold war. Israel, shaky in its foundations, surrounded by a hostile Arab world, terrified about its future, dependent on the economic aid of American Jews, allied itself in fact, if not quite explicitly in words, with the United States. This could not but provoke hostility from Russia. When Mrs. Golda Meir, the first Ambassador of the newly created State arrived in Moscow, Russian Jews greeted her with jubilation and loudly demonstrated their solidarity with Israel. Stalin, who might have watched the unusual scene from his window in the Kremlin, decided that the Jews were an unstable element, that Israel had repaid him with ingratitude (which was to some extent true), that the Jews in the Soviet Union were unreliable. Reckoning with the possibility of a conflict with the U.S.A., or even of a war between Russia and the West, he started to persecute the Jews denouncing them as people 'without a Fatherland', without roots, and again as 'cosmopolitans'. Every Jew, it was whispered, had a relative in the West, most often in America. How could he be trusted as a truly Russian patriot? Could one be absolutely confident that in an emergency his allegiance would lie with the Soviet State? Such was undoubtedly the Stalinist viewpoint.

Analysing objectively and soberly the whole situation as it presented itself in the atmosphere of the cold war, one must admit that this kind of reasoning, alien as it is to me, was not completely devoid of logic. The Jews in Russia had a *penchant*, so to speak, for America and for their relatives there. If one could imagine, for instance, American armies marching into Russia, as the German armies had, they would probably have found a great deal of sympathy and quite a few collaborators among the local Jews. There is no need to deny this. What Stalin, in his crudity, never asked himself was the most fundamental question: How is it that so many decades after the revolution there were still people in Russia whose loyalty to the Soviet régime could be in doubt? If it were true that they were 'unreliable', then perhaps not the Jews should have been blamed but the Soviet government? Even if Stalin had asked himself this question, would he have ever admitted that it was his rule, his perversion of the revolution, that was at fault?

However, this was a very tangled knot of responsibilities, distrust, and fear. In Stalin's hands any political initiative tended to reach extremes of absurdity, brutality, and recklessness. And so the whole world was treated to a sordid spectacle when Stalin staged the so-called 'Doctors' Plot'. On 3 January 1953 it was announced that nine professors of medicine, employed as house doctors to the rulers in the Kremlin, were suddenly arrested and thrown into jail. They were accused of having poisoned some of their illustrious patients; of planning further assassinations, of attempts on the lives of Soviet Marshals and Generals in order to weaken the country's defences; of acting at one and the same time in the interests, and on behalf, of British and American Secret Services and the Jewish international organization, the *Joint*. There were dark hints about imminent further revelations of the scope and ramifications of the plots and of other iniquities of the conspirators. The campaign unleashed against the Jews was, according to some versions, to have ended in the evacuation of all the Jews from their places of residence and in a compulsory re-settlement somewhere in the Far East or in Birobidjan.

Like so many other sinister and pernicious plans hatched by Stalin in the last year of his life, this one too broke down at the moment of his death. The process of de-Stalinization began. The very first move of the new government of Georgi Malenkov, who was then both the First Secretary of the Party and the Prime Minister, was to declare the so-called 'Doctors' Plot' null and void.

With Stalin's death the Soviet Union entered into a new phase. And again the constant tug of war between nationalism and internationalism became strikingly evident. Stalin's death was followed by a reaction against his chauvinistic nationalist and anti-semitic line and by an upsurge of internationalism. But it was not the final, the decisive victory of internationalism which would have defeated all nationalism once and for all. Far from it. There has been for years something like a shaky balance between the two trends; and the balance, tipped one way and then the other, has been producing all those inconsistencies and zigzags which we have been witnessing in the Soviet Union. The whole Khrushchev interregnum was marked by ambiguity in the treatment of the Jewish problem. The anti-semitism of the last years of the Stalin era has gone. The equality of the Jews is upheld. But there is still, according to all accounts, a fairly strong undercurrent of anti-semitism. The truly candid treatment of the Jewish problem is not yet in sight. We cannot hope for it until all other problems of Russia's rich, tragic, inspiring and repulsive past and present are submitted to a free and frank examination by Soviet rulers, Soviet citizens, and communists at large.

# IV

# Remnants of a Race[1]

*'Lt.-Gen. Sir Frederick Morgan, chief of UNRRA operations in Germany and former deputy chief of staff to General Eisenhower, said in Frankfurt that he had seen an exodus of Jews from Poland: all of them were well dressed, well fed, healthy, and had "pockets bulging with money". All of them, he said, told the same monotonous story of threats, pogroms, and atrocities in Poland as reason for their leaving. He did not know who was financing the movement or stuffing Jewish pockets . . . He believed that a "world organization of Jews was being formed" and that Jews had a "positive plan for a second exodus"—this time from Europe.'* The Times, 3 January 1946.

GENERAL Sir Frederick Morgan's statement has turned the limelight on the state of the Jewish problem in Europe to-day. It is a pity that both his statement and the indignant replies to it have been conducted in such sensational and melodramatic language. General Morgan must certainly have had some reason for speaking of an organized plan for a Jewish exodus—the evidence for its existence can indeed be seen in Berlin in the form of thousands of Jews arriving from eastern Europe. Had he confined himself to stating this fact and to an emphatic and urgent warning against the trouble which the 'exodus' was creating for the Allied Military Governments in Germany and for the Jews themselves, nobody could have taken exception to his statement. It may

[1] *The Economist*, 12 January 1946.

well be that his words were in fact intended to carry some such warning—a possibility for which his more violent critics have made no allowance at all. But even so, the form of the warning was most unfortunate. It conveyed the suggestion that the Jews, their pockets stuffed with notes, were repeating the tricks they once played on the Egyptians in their first great Exodus, when, it is related, they borrowed

> every man of his neighbour, and every woman of her neighbour, jewels of silver, and jewels of gold.

It suggested, too, that they had once again evaded the normal barriers and frontier divisions—once with the connivance of the Almighty crossing the Red Sea, now with the connivance of the Russians entering the British zone. In a word, it attributed to the Jews the worst motives in a flight for which many perfectly normal reasons can be given.

European Jewry's desire for a new exodus is undeniable. Zionist organizations, especially of the extremer kind, are stimulating it; and they are trying to force its pace before the survivors of European Jewry again strike root in their old countries. They act in this way from a conviction that the Jews will in any case be prevented from re-establishing themselves permanently in their old communities. They act, in short, on the basis of a deep disbelief in the prospect of a tolerant and civilized Europe, a disbelief unhappily confirmed by continuing manifestations of violent anti-semitism on the continent. These cannot be denied, though they are magnified by Jewish fear and panic. Travellers returning from Poland and the Danubian area, reports in the press of those countries, and statements by officials leave no doubt at all that the atmosphere of eastern Europe is still infested with virulent anti-semitism.

The issue transcends in importance the Morgan incident and even the administrative inconveniences which the influx of Jews to Germany is causing to the Military Governments. Anti-semitism invariably reflects or foreshadows a diseased condition in European civilization. Its rise and fall is perhaps the most sensitive index of Europe's moral and political sanity. The Jew was the first victim of the orgy of Nazi madness and destruction that was to engulf the whole continent. It might have been thought that after the holocaust of the last few years the Jews would now have the right to expect sympathy and human understanding from their countrymen and the world at large. The fact that anti-semitism is nevertheless rampant in eastern Europe, and certainly on the increase, though still only latent, in western Europe, is therefore all the more an alarming symptom of social and political disintegration.

The emancipation of the Jews in the nineteenth century followed middle-class liberalism in its spread across Europe. The first declaration of equal rights for Jews, the first one in the whole history of Christian civilization, was made by Jacobin France in 1791. 'Let the Jews look for their Jerusalem in France'—was Napoleon's enlightened maxim. He was hardly a sentimentalist about the Jews; and there was a tyrant's touch in his policy towards them; for instance, he seriously proposed that every third Jew or Jewess should be compelled to marry a Christian. But his purpose of disaccustoming the Jews from usury and illicit trade, of breaking down their separatism and making them submerge themselves in the gentile population was certainly sound; and—who knows?—if it had been consistently carried into effect all over Europe, the Jewish problem might have been forgotten long ago; and our generation would perhaps have been spared the indelible shame of witnessing the deliberate murder of six million human beings in concentration camps and gas chambers.

The emancipation of the Jews in the greater part of Germany was also a by-product of the Napoleonic conquest. The triumph of reaction on the continent under the Holy Alliance deprived the Jews of most of their newly won rights. For individual Jews baptism then became once again the passport to European civilization, until the 'Spring of the Peoples' of 1848 came to give a strong new stimulus to Jewish emancipation, at least in western Europe. So strongly was Jewish emancipation bound up with the spread of middle-class liberalism (though not necessarily with the existence of strictly liberal Governments) that where the influence of that liberalism failed to spread, the Jews never obtained equal rights. The power of the middle classes and their liberal ideas weakened steadily from western to eastern Europe. The non-Jewish middle classes of Russia, Poland, and Rumania (the countries in which the bulk of European Jewry lived) were themselves too weak and too deeply enmeshed in feudal backwardness and racial prejudice to champion equal rights for the Jews, who were often their competitors. What bourgeois liberalism achieved for Jews in western Europe, only Bolshevism was able to achieve for them in eastern Europe. The Communists, admittedly, would not permit Jews to continue as capitalists or 'unproductive elements', but otherwise gave them equal rights.

It was in Poland and Rumania with their four million Jews that the Jewish issue was most acute before the war. Much more than in other countries, and even in Germany, anti-semitism was a popular movement. It embodied all sorts of moods and motives: the jealousy felt by the underdeveloped Polish middle classes for their Jewish rivals and competitors; the socialism of the ignorant and especially of the *déclassé*, in which the Jews were blamed as a sinister and mysterious capitalist power; the deeply rooted clerical hatred of the Jew as 'Christ's enemy'; and, finally, the fear of all Governments of Communism spreading among the vast mass of utterly impoverished Jewish artisans and outright paupers. The gentile working classes and the peasantry in those countries, on the whole, remained unaffected by persistent anti-semitic propaganda. But they also remained aloof from the Jews and more or less indifferent to their fate. The gulf of separatism between Jew and gentile was, at least in part, responsible for the uncanny passivity and indifference with which the mass of gentiles watched the apocalyptic slaughter of the Jews.

Nor is this the whole of the picture. The grave of the Jewish middle class became the cradle of a new gentile middle class in eastern Europe. At the height of the slaughter a Polish paper wrote: 'The Nazis are solving the Jewish problem in our favour in a way in which we could never have solved it.' Jewish shops, houses, flats and personal belongings were seized by Poles, Rumanians and Hungarians. These profiteers were the most demoralized, greedy and unscrupulous elements in those nations—a *lumpenproletariat* which turned overnight into a *lumpenbourgeoisie*. The death certificates of the murdered Jews were their only valid trade licences. These new 'middle classes' are undoubtedly suffering from a guilt complex which makes their temper extremely nervous and brutal. They look tensely and anxiously into the faces of the few Jews who now seek to return home. Has the rightful owner of the shop come back? Or his child or relative? The greater the destitution in eastern

Europe, the wilder the scramble for material goods, the more desperate and unscrupulous the determination of this horrible 'middle class' to remain in possession. Possession is in any event nine-tenths of the law—zoological anti-semitism provides the last tenth. The only way in which the new 'middle class' can save not so much its newly acquired wealth but its nerves and a pretence of respectability is by smoking out the surviving Jews.

This is surely the most morbid feature in the life of eastern Europe today. Woe to eastern Europe if this social hyena class were ever to become its ruling class! The blacker aspects of the present Russian-controlled régimes would pale in comparison with the horrors which this class could hold in store not so much for the Jews (for they have very little left to lose) as for the peoples of eastern Europe. This class forms the hard core of the anti-Russian opposition in each country. They are now the cadres of the various terroristic organizations and are ready to be the most brutal and determined element of any eastern European counter-revolution. The recent outbursts of anti-semitic violence are merely a warning of quite a different violence that may yet threaten the peace in that part of the world.

Meanwhile, what has the civilized world to offer the survivors of Belsen, Auschwitz, Dachau, and Majdanek? After the first World War it offered the Jews two hopes: the Balfour Declaration on the Jewish Home in Palestine and the Protection of Minorities by the League of Nations. The Protection of Minorities has proved to be a scrap of paper. The scheme for a Jewish Home has met—as could easily have been foreseen—with the overwhelming opposition of the Arab world. Is it possible that the great, democratic nations of the world should have become so helpless that they cannot offer the Jews a strip of land somewhere on the globe or a few hundred thousand entry visas to their countries? Or have they perhaps become so poor that they can make no gesture of charity to the worst wrecks and victims of this war—the remnants of an extraordinary, an unhappy, but not completely negligible race?

# V

# Israel's Spiritual Climate[1]

WHAT is an Israeli and what is a Jew? This question is much discussed in Israel, because the relationship between Israel and the Jews of the world is of obvious importance to the young state. Many Zionists believe in *Kibbutz Hagaluth*, the return of Jewry from all the countries of the Diaspora. In their eyes every Jew outside Israel is virtually an exile; he has his duties towards Israel, the ultimate duty being to become an Israeli citizen. Young Israelis, on the other hand, especially the *Sabras*, born and brought up in the country, have no sense of 'belonging to world Jewry', and, consequently, they do not see 'world Jewry' as belonging to Israel. Some of them go so far as to say that they are Israelis, not Jews.

The distinction is perhaps not quite unreal. There is a touch of un-Jewishness about Israel: about the farmers struggling with the desert and making patches of it into vineyards and olive groves; about the soldiers cold-bloodedly watching the Arabs across the frontiers; about the popular consciousness of statehood and the toughness with which the people are willing to defend their State against the outside world.

'Don't you feel that we, Jews, have our roots here?' the

[1] *The Reporter*, April–May 1954.

visitor is asked. These words 'roots' and 'rootlessness' occur very often in conversation. The ex-inmate of Nazi concentration camps, the sufferer from the old Polish anti-semitism, and the victim of the Rumanian Iron Guard at last has the feeling of being at home and secure. He expresses his satisfaction, relief, and pride.

All too often, however, a shrill overtone of nationalist mysticism jars on one's ears, a mysticism which is not free of the old Chosen-People-racialism and which accords badly with the element of cool rationalism in the Jewish mind. But, after all, Israel is the country of the *Zohar*, that second Bible of the world's mystics, and the homeland of the *Kabbalists* who spun their visions on the colourful rocks of nearby Safed . . . All the same, there is something disquieting in the intensity of the nationalist emotion that creeps into talks with Israelis, from the Prime Minister down to the road-mender.

Ben Gurion speaks to me bitterly about non-Zionist Jews: 'They have no roots, they are *rootless cosmopolitans*— there can be nothing worse than that.' I remark that he speaks as Stalin's propagandists until recently spoke about Jews at large. He waves his hands in protest:

'No, no. As Prime Minister of this country I have always maintained that, in order to be of full value to their own State, Israelis must feel that they are citizens of the world— I am not inveighing against "rootless cosmopolitanism" in the way they did in Moscow.'

This is, of course, Ben Gurion's second thought. Instinctively he condemns and denounces all those non-Zionist Jews in whom 'belonging to Jewry' is not a central idea or a dominant emotion. But when attention is drawn to some coincidence between his words and Stalinist propaganda (of the era of 'the doctors' plot'), he blushes with embarrassment and corrects himself.

In Israel the oldest people in the world have formed the youngest nation-state; and they are emotionally anxious to make good the time lost. To nearly all the Jews here the ideal of individual and collective happiness is to grow a solid, protective national shell. This implies getting rid of the Diaspora, the memories, the habits, the tastes, and the smells of exile—millennia of exile. It implies forgetting the climates, the landscapes, the melodies, and the languages of so many countries: Poland, Russia, Lithuania, Austria, Morocco, Turkey, and Iraq. What a complex and many-sided process of psychological self-uprooting following upon tragic processes of physical displacement. In fact the overwhelming majority of this generation of Israelis has struck no roots in Israel and cannot strike any. Israel is the State of the displaced person; and that is why they talk so much about 'striking roots'.

They crave to get away from their past and to put out of their mind all the marks of indignity, all the stigmata of shame, all the yellow patches that Jew-hatred has ever devised. They even crave to put out of their mind part of their own mind. Some Israelis, for instance, feel almost neurotically ashamed of Yiddish, the language of their first nursery rhymes and first Bible stories, the 'jargon' in which an amazingly rich literature grew up in Eastern Europe before Jewry's catastrophe. On board an Israeli ship or in Tel Aviv I approach a stranger and ask in what language he should be addressed: often the answer is: German; only very rarely it is Yiddish. But the moment the stranger opens his mouth it is obvious that he speaks Yiddish—of German proper he has almost no knowledge. But he will not admit it: Yiddish is the linguistic 'yellow patch' he is determined to discard.

This attitude towards Yiddish was, however, characteristic of Zionism long before Hitler. From its beginning Zionism has aimed at the revival of Hebrew. There is a certain snobbery about it as there would be in an attempt by Greeks or Italians to abandon their modern languages and to revert to the classical Greek or Latin. Zionism has always seen Jewry as the fairy-tale prince who has been condemned to live in pauperism for many years, but then returns to his royal palace, discards the grey and dirty rags of the painful masquerade, and puts on his royal gold and purple. At the threshold of Israel Jewry thus abandons the rags of Yiddish for the gold and purple of Hebrew.

'When are you going to start writing your books in Hebrew instead of English?' Ben Gurion asks me in a tone of suggestive self-confidence—he takes it for granted that any Jewish-born writer is under a moral obligation towards Israel's Hebrew literature.

This Israeli-Hebrew self-assertiveness is calculated to weld all the disparate elements of Israel into a single nation and to give that nation a spiritual and cultural unity. However, behind this self-assertiveness there is also the Jews' natural nostalgia after the countries and cultures of their childhood and youth, a nostalgia which sometimes expresses itself in forms of the utmost nobility.

Almost every window of an Israeli bookshop tells you the tale of that nostalgia—almost every such window is a Jewish intellectual elegy. The bookshop is an extremely important element in Israeli life, for the Jews here have remained the *Am Hassefer*—the 'People of the Book'. The book is a first necessity here; and in Tel Aviv, Haifa or

Jerusalem there seem to be as many bookshops and lending libraries as there are grocery and greengrocery stores. In the farming settlements there are rich libraries the like of which you will hardly find in any countryside elsewhere.

It is not the crime-and-sex-story, the comic strip, or the cheap best-seller that fills the shelves, but the great and serious books of the poets and thinkers and social visionaries of all nations. You find them here in Hebrew translations and in their original languages. In one window, for instance, of a smallish backstreet bookshop I find an elaborate edition of Goethe in German, a new Hebrew translation of Heine's *Buch der Lieder*, new Israeli editions of Gogol and Pushkin next to Hebrew translations of Freud's works, a selection of Walt Whitman's poems and a new Hebrew rendering of Mickiewicz's *Pan Tadeusz*, Poland's national epic, and some Hungarian and Rumanian novels. Every group of immigrants seems anxious to convey the artistic thrills and literary excitements of its own childhood and youth to children brought up in Israel. A former Leipzig lawyer would like his son to taste with him the richness of Nietzsche's style; a Polish Jewess cannot imagine her daughter growing up without reading the social-patriotic novels of Żeromski; and an old Jew of Odessa argues with his grandson over the profundity of *The Brothers Karamazov*.

Heinrich Heine once wrote that the Jews, when they were driven from their land, left behind them all their riches and took into exile only one possession—the Book. Then over the centuries that 'phantom of a people' stood guard over the Book, the Bible, preserving it for the rest of mankind. Now the 'phantom' again materializes into a nation; and as it returns to its country it brings home to the banks of the Jordan and the Hills of Judea all the great books of the nations of the world.

*        *        *

The State of Israel has been the work primarily of the Jews of Eastern Europe, especially of Russia, Poland, and Lithuania. From their ranks came nearly all the visionaries of Zionism, except Herzl and Nordau, nearly all the early leaders, spokesmen, statesmen, and pioneers. In 1948, when the Jewish State was proclaimed, Jews of Russian and Polish stock formed about one half of its population.

It was in the Eastern European ghettoes that the ancient current of Jewish life ran strongest and that Jews dreamt the dreams of Zion most intensely. When on Passover they greeted each other with the traditional *Leshono habo be Yerushalaim*—'Next year in Jerusalem'—the greeting sounded very differently there from the way it sounded in Jewish homes in Western Europe or America. The processes by which before the rise of Nazism French, British, Italian, and German Jews were being 'assimilated' never went far in Russia and Poland. The Jews there lived in large and compact masses; they had their own homogeneous way of life; and the absorptive powers of the Slavonic cultures were anyhow too weak to draw them in and assimilate them. Eastern Europe was therefore the land of Jewry *par excellence* (not for nothing was Vilna called 'the Jerusalem of Lithuania'). Is it to be wondered at that Israel is, as one Jew of Western European origin puts it, a 'spiritual colony of the East European ghetto'?

Yet the East European ghetto had been deeply divided against itself; it had been in revolt against itself, against its own orthodoxy and tradition, and against the outside world.

That revolt took the two rival forms of Zionism and revolutionary-Marxist socialism.

While in the West socialism, liberalism, and Zionism were benevolently related to one another, in Eastern Europe they bitterly competed for the loyalty of the Jewish masses. A deep cleavage always existed there between the Zionist and the anti-Zionist Jew. The anti-Zionist urged the Jews to trust their gentile environment, to help the 'progressive forces' in that environment to come to the top, and so hope that those forces would effectively defend the Jews against anti-semitism. 'Social revolution will give the Jews equality and freedom; they have therefore no need for a Zionist Messiah', this was the stock argument of generations of Jewish left-wingers. The Zionists, on the other hand, dwelt on the deep-seated hatred of non-Jews towards Jews and urged the Jews to trust their future to nobody except their own State. In this controversy Zionism has scored a horrible victory, one which it could neither wish nor expect: six million Jews had to perish in Hitler's gas chambers in order that Israel should come to life. It would have been better had Israel remained unborn and the six million Jews stayed alive—but who can blame Zionism and Israel for the different outcome? Israel is more than a spiritual colony of the Eastern European ghettoes. It is their great, tragic, posthumous offspring fighting for survival with breathtaking vitality.

Eastern European Zionism was implicitly anti-revolutionary. Nevertheless it breathed the air of the Russian revolution, the air of that vast movement of revolutionary ideas which preceded the Bolshevik revolution and reached its culmination with that revolution. On Zionism that movement of ideas left an indelible mark.

The young Jew who in Kiev, Odessa, and Warsaw distrusted the Russo-Polish revolutionary ideologies and longed to pioneer for the Jewish State in Palestine was as a rule hypnotised by the ideologies from which he fled; and he found this out after he had landed in Palestine. He came to Palestine with the crumbs from the table of the Russian revolution; and he used those crumbs as the seed with which to sow the sacred desert of Galilee, Samaria, and Judea.

At the new, imposing Tel Aviv headquarters of the Histadruth[1] some of the leaders are more at ease when they speak Russian than when they speak any other language, although they emigrated from Russia more than thirty years ago. Ben Gurion had no sooner welcomed me than he launched out on a lecture on the Russian revolution—the topic obviously fascinated him:

'One man', he said, 'could have saved the world, but, unfortunately, he missed his opportunity. That man was Lenin.'

Ben Gurion is a Polish rather than a Russian Jew; but this naive dictum is his unwitting tribute to the Russian revolution.

Mordehai Namir, the Secretary General of Histadruth, when asked about the guiding organization-principle of Histadruth, answers with unshakeable confidence:

'The governing principle here is democratic centralism—don't you know it?'

Democratic centralism, in the strict sense is, of course, not a Russian or Bolshevik invention—it came to Russian and the Bolsheviks from Western Europe. But it has come to Israel and Histadruth from Russia.

There are in Israel some striking contrasts of wealth and poverty. The distance between the hovels of the *Maabara*

[1] Israeli Trade Union Congress.

transit camps for moneyless immigrants and the luxurious hotels and villas on Mount Carmel is very great indeed. But there is also a widespread and acute sense of shame for these contrasts, a sense of shame such as existed in the Russia of Tolstoy and Chekhov. There is an egalitarian spirit alive in the working class such as flourished in Soviet Russia before it was eradicated by Stalinism. The trade unions stick to a quasi-egalitarian wage policy. The pay packets of the skilled and unskilled workers, the office employee, the professional man, and the civil servant differ relatively little in size; and people grumble that lack of incentive payment is retarding Israel's economic progress.

The kibbutz, the rural commune, is the epitome of Israeli egalitarianism. It is also the most important feature of Israel's moral and intellectual landscape. The kibbutz is an indirect descendant of an idea of the Russian *Narodniks* or Populists; and it is a *Narodnik* vision of rural socialism that seems to have materialized in the Jewish oases scattered over the former Arabian desert.

The *Narodniks* preached their agrarian socialism in the second half of the last century when Russia did not yet possess any modern industry; and the 'Lovers of Zion', the forerunners of modern Zionism, came from Russia to Palestine before the Narodnik Utopia had faded completely. The next *Aliyah* (immigration-wave) came after the defeat of the Russian revolution of 1905–6; and the men of that *Aliyah* founded some of the greatest and most beautiful kibbutzim in Galilee, near Tiberias, and in the hills of Judea, on the approaches to Jerusalem. The next phalanx of immigrants arrived after the Bolshevik revolution. The rich Russian Jews who emigrating managed to save some of their wealth settled in Berlin, Paris, or London. Those who came to Palestine strove to save only their dream of the Jewish State.

In Russia, under the New Economic Policy, Lenin's government encouraged a handful of idealistic peasants and party intellectuals to form voluntary, experimental rural communes which were cherished as 'laboratories of the future' and which should not be confused with the collective farms of the Stalin era. The new kibbutzim in Israel were modelled on those early Russian communes. They were built by boys and girls who left their parental homes, and enlisted in radical Zionist socialist organizations, like *Hashomer Hatzair*, not in order to fight class struggles but in order to drain the marshes of the Emek and of Huleh and to cover the slopes of Carmel and Samaria with the green of vineyards and orchards.

Sociologically, the kibbutz is a unique institution. Its antecedents go back even further than to the old Russian Populism. They may be found in Fourier's blueprints of the *phalanstères*, in Robert Owen's co-operative experiments, and in other brilliantly erratic schemes of the classical age of Utopian socialism. Like the Utopian socialists, the founders of the kibbutz hoped to achieve socialism by personal example rather than by any systematic revolutionary overthrow of established society—and, incidentally, no established society existed in the Palestine desert. The castles in the air built by Utopian socialism usually collapsed as soon as they were erected. The kibbutz is built literally on sand; but it has shown much more solidity. The oldest of the kibbutzim will soon celebrate their half century jubilee, and there are many that are twenty or thirty years old, and have grown in prosperity and achievement.

He who has not seen the kibbutz can hardly imagine the boldness and originality of the idea and of its execution. A kibbutz has usually several hundred members, living in small flats which are sometimes very aesthetically built and furnished. Opposite rows of white bungalows surrounded by flower beds are the common dining rooms, libraries, schools, the medical point and other buildings of public utility, with workshops and farmsheds on the fringes of the settlement. The division of labour among kibbutz members is voluntary; and it grows more and more elaborate with progress in agricultural technology. In some kibbutzim there are auxiliary factories of considerable size. Working hours are nine for members under fifty, four for older ones. If a member shows artistic or scientific inclinations, the board of the commune may shorten his working hours on the farm, or give him a Sabbatical year.

Rewards in kind are the same for all. Food, clothing, furniture, medical supplies, cigarettes, books (even paintings or artistic reproductions) are all distributed from a common pool—'to each according to his needs'. Every member gets a few pounds of pocket money. The standard of living of a kibbutz depends on the size of the common pool, i.e. on wealth accumulated over the years, on productivity of current work, and on the profit made by the marketing organization which sells the surpluses of production to outsiders.

The communist principle has been boldly extended to the education of children, who are brought up within the kibbutz but live in their own quarters and spend with their parents only a couple of leisure hours in the evening. I have noticed that members of the kibbutz are so used to the communal upbringing of the children that in quite a natural, unaffected manner they speak of all the children in their kibbutz as they speak of their own children.

The kibbutz is in some ways a combination of the scout camp and the Benedictine monastery, brightened up by the lack of coercive discipline and by ease and purposefulness of human relations. The members of the kibbutz have every reason to be proud of their morale and they are quite conscious of it. They tell you that during the war the Soviet diplomatic envoy in Israel and his staff visited many kibbutzim trying to see how they compared with Soviet collective farms. Not unnaturally the comparison worked against the Soviet *kolkhozy*, which had depended on a backward, sluggish, and intimidated *muzhik*, whereas the kibbutzim had been built by the self-sacrifice and courage of idealistic intellectuals and workers. In one kibbutz, having inspected the modern dairy, the school, the farm library (composed of what used to be the libraries of twenty German university professors), the dramatic circle, and so on, the Soviet envoy asked to be shown the kibbutz prison.

'We have no prison here,' was the reply.

'Impossible!' the diplomat exclaimed, 'How on earth do you deal with criminals or offenders?'

The kibbutz members tried to explain that so far they had not had to deal with any offence grave enough to call for such punishment; and that this was only natural: members were selected with the utmost care; they were men and women of high socialist morality; the discontented were free to leave; and in extreme cases the kibbutz could expel unsuitable members. That particular kibbutz was dominated by the pro-Stalinist Mapam party; but the Soviet envoy refused to believe what he was told:

'Surely', said he, 'a community of several hundred people cannot do without a jail!'

The Russian did not conceal his incredulity; and he

intimated that he thought it a good joke that for once Jews should show their own Potemkin village to a Russian.

However, only about seventy thousand people, not more than five per cent of Israel's population, live in kibbutzim. These are Israel's Pilgrim Fathers. Their influence is much greater than their numbers. In the towns you meet many people who have belonged to a kibbutz at one time or another and who still respond to its idealistic appeal; and many town dwellers are anxious to send their children to kibbutz schools famous for ultra-modern educational methods.

Under the British Mandate the weight of the kibbutz in Palestine's life was much greater than it is now. The Jewish population was much smaller then. No machinery of Jewish government, no Jewish army, police or judiciary existed and the kibbutz, with its solid organization and high morale and discipline, formed a kind of a Jewish shadow State. Many present civil servants and officers have come from the kibbutz and have as a rule remained members of their rural commune. Some try to combine service to the State with work for the kibbutz. This is possible only because of the smallness of the State and of the somewhat tribal character of Israeli society. In one kibbutz, for example, I discovered that the tractor driver was formerly Israel's ambassador in Prague and Budapest. In another, I was shown a tall, strong, sunburnt and bare-foot shepherd (with almost a family likeness to Michelangelo's David), driving sheep from the fields in a golden sunset; and I was told that this was one of the commanders of the Israeli army during the 'war of emancipation' of 1948.

The kibbutz is still Israel's moral power station, but for some time now it has been in the throes of a crisis. It has been overshadowed by the newly fledged State and swamped by the influx of new immigrants. The pioneers of Zionism share the sad lot of so many other pioneers: they are defeated by their very success.

Since 1948 the population of Israel has more than doubled. The newcomers are not like the idealists of the previous *Aliyahs*; they are the wrecks of concentration camps, the flotsam and jetsam of European Jewry, and the masses of Oriental Jews, refugees from Arab hatred and revenge. To many new immigrants the ideals of the Zionist Pilgrim Fathers are alien and incomprehensible. A little rickety junk shop or a tobacconist's stand somewhere in town seems to them a thousand times more desirable and respectable than all the collectivist wonders of the kibbutz and than even its relatively high standard of living. Tens of thousands of these new immigrants still live on the dole in the sub-slums of the transit camps. Some of them even refuse to move into new blocks of flats built for them by the government. They prefer to go on living on the dole in their old hovels than to pay rent in the new house. A few re-emigrate to Tunis or Morocco. The country's economy can absorb them only slowly and painfully, if at all. In vain does the kibbutz invite them to join its ranks as equal members.

'We are townspeople; we are not going to become country bumpkins!' answer former tailors of Bucharest and peddlers of Vilna.

'We wish to earn our own money, to put aside some savings. We believe in property—not for us your common ownership!' say some.

'We do not want', say others, 'to eat in public dining rooms all our lives and to have our children separated from us.'

'Employ us as your workers and wage earners,' yet others ask 'but pay us cash and do not demand that we become members of your commune!'

This is worse than an insult to kibbutz faith—it also creates (or perhaps only brings to light) a new moral dilemma. The kibbutz finds itself confronted by a demand that it should become a 'capitalist employer'; and, strangely, it is from would-be workers and employees that the demand comes. For the kibbutz to hire labour would be to abandon and betray its first principle. So, at any rate, the mass of members feel even in those kibbutzim which adhere to the moderate socialism of Mapai. On the other hand, the government headed by the Mapai leaders, is anxious to settle the new immigrants and urges the kibbutz to give up 'ideological purism' and to hire idle labour from the transit camps. Voices asking for the same come also from inside the kibbutz. The economy of the farming communes has expanded strongly in recent years but their membership has tended to remain stationary. Outside labour has to be hired in order to sustain expansion and prevent stagnation. 'To hire or not to hire?' is *the* moral issue now passionately debated. Some breaches have already been made in the fortresses of common ownership: you run into groups of hired labourers within the boundaries of many a kibbutz. The theoreticians work hard to devise new formulas designed to limit the amount of hired labour; and all kibbutzim 'from Dan to Beersheba' take a solemn oath never to become capitalist businesses no matter how high the flood of capitalism outside their walls.

Thus the story of the *phalanstères* may, after all, be repeating itself in Israel. All the business experiments of Utopian socialism either collapsed or transformed themselves into efficient capitalist enterprises. This may be the ultimate lot of the kibbutz as well, unless some social upheaval in the Middle East changes the broader environment of the kibbutz.

For the time being the kibbutz struggles to hold its ground, and it is helped in this by the fact that it serves an important national interest. It is still the chief bulwark of Israel's defence. It bore the brunt of the war of independence, fighting its vanguard and its rearguard battles. The structure of its organization makes of the kibbutz an ideal military colony and militia. In every kibbutz they lead you to the local cemetery, showing the graves of their husbands and brothers, killed in action against the Arabs and the stirring monuments to the fallen erected by local (sometimes world-famous) sculptors. If you happen to arrive at a kibbutz after dusk, the sentry who stops you, Sten-gun in hand, at the kibbutz gate is likely to be a girl of eighteen. Most of the kibbutzim are close to the frontier, and on them the Israeli government bases militarily as well as morally all its plans of defence.

The bastions of Israel's Utopian socialism bristle with Sten-guns.

\*     \*     \*

The cultural outlook of Israel is strongly affected by changes in the composition of the people. Under the British Mandate Jews of European origin formed the overwhelming majority. Now they are only a minority. Immigrants from Asia and Africa constitute over fifty per cent of the people of Israel.

Jews from French North Africa, half Arab and half French in outlook, vociferous and turbulent, sit with their families in front of their huts and shops taken over from

Arabs. The parents talk shop and argue over the pros and cons of a return journey to Morocco or Tunisia; while their children read and discuss the latest issue of *Nouvelles Littéraires* of Paris. Then there are the Jews of Iran in black lambskin hats, and those of Iraq, and of Turkey, some Westernized, others Oriental; and the Bukhara Jews in white, flowing, silken Sabbath-dress and with soft biblical beards. Finally, there are the Yemenites with black glowing eyes and black, long, curled sidelocks dangling from shaven heads. Their girls crowd the open-air labour-markets seeking work as domestic servants.

The story is told how the British airways brought over to Israel forty-five thousand Yemenites, men, women, and children. They gaily boarded the planes which they had never seen before: they believed that these were the 'wings of the White Eagle' on which, according to an old prophesy, they were destined to return to the Holy Land when Messiah came. But on landing they were frightened to death when they were told to board buses that were to take them from the Israeli airport to the transit camps: there was nothing in the Messianic prophesy about vehicles like buses.

The Jews here are no longer only Europe's overspill into Asia, which they were for so many years—the Levant and the Southern Arabian desert have made their contributions to Israel. But how will this meeting of Orient and Occident affect Israel's cultural outlook? In Jerusalem and Tel Aviv one hears all sorts of profound theories and prognostications. Some point to the very high birthrate of Oriental Jews and predict the eventual Orientalization of Israel. Others foresee a 'synthesis' and a new Israeli culture. I suppose that the European Jews will eventually assimilate the Oriental ones. They represent the higher civilization which usually 'conquers' the lower; and they are already conquering it through school and army, both of decisive importance for the unification of Israel's language, culture, and custom.

In the meantime a certain antagonism between the Oriental and the Western Jew is noticeable. The Western Jew holds all the positions of influence in civil service, army, education, industry, commerce, and finance. The Eastern Jew feels himself a second-class citizen, a victim of discrimination and European arrogance. (In some cases he even complains of a colour bar.) Grievances so long voiced by Jew against gentile are voiced here by Jew against Jew. Some of the Oriental Jews find that their social status is lower than in their old country. For instance, in French North Africa the Jewish trader stood half-way between the *colon* and the backward Arab—he was somewhere in the middle of the social ladder. In Israel he is down at the bottom: *vis-à-vis* the European Jew he is in a position similar to that in which the North African Arab finds himself *vis-à-vis* the Frenchman.

The European Jew is aware of the Orientals' jealousy and resentment and is sometimes afraid of them. You can even hear doubts expressed about their loyalty:

'Goodness knows, in case of trouble they may even join hands with the Arabs. There isn't much difference between them and the Arabs, is there?'

This is probably not a view seriously held, but it does indicate tension. Some think that one day the animosity of the Oriental Jews may be whipped up and exploited, for instance, by the Revisionists, the potential fascist party, whose strength for the time being is negligible. In the meantime all parties and leaders make their moves with one eye on the Oriental half of the nation, trying to gauge its sensibilities and to influence its morale. When high officials argue that a tough policy has to be adopted towards the Arabs because Oriental people are likely to take any other policy as a sign of weakness, they have in mind not only the Arabs but the Oriental Israelis as well. The 'acts of retaliation' against the Arabs, including the Kibiya massacre, were calculated as much to keep up the spirit of the Oriental Israelis as to intimidate the Arabs.

Most of the Oriental Jews are orthodox in religious matters and sometimes follow the lead of fanatical East European rabbis. This was the case in the riotous demonstrations against the introduction of auxiliary military service for women. Yet the orthodoxy of the African and Asian Jews is inspired more by social conservatism than by religious bigotry; it is at any rate milder and more tolerant than the orthodoxy of the European Jews. The Polish, Russian, and Lithuanian rabbis, wonderrabbis and their adherents are among the world's wildest religious fanatics; and their haunts in Mea Shaarim—'The Hundred Gates'— form a genuine reservation of the Jewish Middle Ages.

Despite the name, suggesting romantic-Oriental antiquity, The Hundred Gates date back only to the last century. It was in that quarter of Jerusalem that old and pious Jews settled when they came to Palestine in order to die in the Holy Land. At every time of the day, the slummy, overcrowded rows of tenement houses resound with the chant of prayer and Talmud-reading. There are as many synagogues, Talmud-schools, and shops with liturgical articles at Mea Shaarim as there are dwelling houses. The long-bearded, dark-eyed, and pale-faced inhabitants dress in long black robes even in the worst heat, and so do the little boys who enjoy the blessing of studying the commentators of the Talmud within a stone's throw from Mount Zion. Here the terrible maxim of the Mishna is still in full force, the maxim according to which it is a grave sin for a Jew to say: 'Look, how lovely is that tree yonder', because the Lord alone should be admired. The men and even the little boys of Mea Shaarim have their gaze turned in upon themselves or downward; and so they avoid casting a sinful glance on the tree or the passing woman. Here the heretic may still be excommunicated at the synagogue to the sound of the ram's horn and by the light of wax candles, for where if not in the vicinity of the biblical Gan Hinom should rabbinical law be enforced in all its strictness?

Every Friday before dusk the zealots of Mea Shaarim occupy the thoroughfare leading from the centre of the town to their quarters. With frantic dancing they welcome the Sabbath and stop all street traffic until the following night. Woe to the passer-by who on a Sabbath ventures into the crooked streets of Mea Shaarim with a pipe in his mouth or holding a girl by the arm. A hail of stones will come down upon him, for Mea Shaarim believes in the biblical stoning of the sinner. And if a doctor in his car or ambulance ventures into these crooked streets on a Sabbath the shower of stones will come down upon him too.

Mea Shaarim is important not because of its exotic 'local colour' but because of its influence upon Israel's cultural climate. That influence should not be underrated: the kibbutz and Mea Shaarim are the two opposite poles of Israel's spiritual life. Jewish 'free thinkers' and 'militant progressives' become very meek when they are left alone with Jewish orthodoxy. And so in Israel the Talmudic law still governs all marriage and family relations, to mention only some of the areas of Jewish life under its domination. Until quite recently an old-fashioned orthodox rabbi, with hardly any secular education, was Dean of the Law Faculty of the University of Jerusalem. At every step one comes across some evidence which supports the charge, already made, that there is much more than a touch of an anachronistic theocracy about Israel.

I discussed this with the editor of a highbrow leftish periodical, a gifted writer and a translator of Shakespeare into Hebrew. He protested with some heat against a remark that Israel was under the spiritual sway of Mea Shaarim. But subjected to questioning he admitted that the Israelis paid considerable tribute to religious orthodoxy. To take one tragi-comic example: they may not breed pigs, although pig breeding could rapidly help to solve Israel's food problem and ease the balance of payment. Keren Kayemeth, the National Fund that owns most of the land, leases it out on the express condition that the tenant will breed no pigs. Thus even the atheistic kibbutzim of the extreme left are made to conform to the will of the rabbis. The editor at first tried to find all sorts of 'progressive' excuses, but then he got red in the face and lost his temper:

'Do you really suggest', he shouted, 'that in order to ease our economic plight *we* should allow pigs to be bred in this Holy Land? Never, never, never!'

\*    \*    \*

Israelis who have known me as an anti-Zionist of long standing are curious to hear what I think about Zionism. I have, of course, long since abandoned my anti-Zionism, which was based on a confidence in the European labour movement, or, more broadly, in European society and civilization, which that society and civilization have not justified. If, instead of arguing against Zionism in the 1920s and 1930s I had urged European Jews to go to Palestine, I might have helped to save some of the lives that were later extinguished in Hitler's gas chambers.

For the remnants of European Jewry—is it only for them?—the Jewish State has become an historic necessity. It is also a living reality. Whatever their cleavages, grievances, and frustrations, the Jews of Israel are animated by a fresh and strong sense of nationhood and by a dogged determination to consolidate and strengthen their State by every means at their disposal. They also have the feeling—how well justified—that the 'civilized world', which in one way or another has the fate of European Jewry on its conscience, has no moral ground to stand on when it tries to sermonize or threaten Israel for any real or imaginary breaches of international commitments.

Even now, however, I am not a Zionist; and I have repeatedly said so in public and in private. The Israelis accept this with unexpected tolerance but seem bewildered:

'How is it possible *not* to embrace Zionism?' they ask, 'if one recognizes the State of Israel as an historic necessity?'

What a difficult and painful question to answer!

From a burning or sinking ship people jump no matter where—on to a lifeboat, a raft, or a float. The jumping is for them an 'historic necessity'; and the raft is in a sense the basis of their whole existence. But does it follow that the jumping should be made into a programme, or that one should take a raft-State as the basis of a political orientation? (I hope that Israelis or Zionists who happen to read this will not misunderstand the expression 'raft-State'. It describes the precariousness of Israel, but is not meant to belittle Israel's constructive achievement.)

To my mind it is just another Jewish tragedy that the world has driven the Jew to seek safety in a nation-state in the middle of this century when the nation-state is falling into decay.

Through several centuries every progressive development in the life of Western nations was bound up with the formation and growth of the nation-state or with the movement for the nation-state. The Jew was not connected with that movement and did not benefit from it. He remained shut up in his synagogue and in his religious loyalties while Western man subordinated religious to national loyalties and found his stature within his nation rather than within his Church. Only now, when man no longer grows in stature within the nation and when he can find himself anew only within some supranational community, has the Jew found his Nation and his State. What a melancholy anachronism!

'Ah, but show us the nation that has abandoned its statehood for the sake of a cosmopolitan or internationalist dream,' say my Israeli friends.

No-one has done so, of course; and it has not occurred to me to urge Israelis to do so. The point is that the nation-state decays and disintegrates whether people are aware of it or not, no matter what their efforts to preserve it. The process is world-wide, however varied its local manifestations. Much of the strength of the Soviet bloc consists in its endeavour to unify economically the area stretching from central Europe to the Chinese Seas and the productive forces of the area's 800 million inhabitants. To achieve this, Stalinism has reduced national sovereignty to a sham, although it has left its outward symbols intact. The nation-states of the West have so far preserved more than symbolic façades; but they, too, have left their golden age far, very far, behind; and their clinging to sovereignty is more often than not a source of their weakness. Like any organism that has outlived its day, the nation-state can prolong its existence only by intensifying all the processes of its own degeneration. In the Third Reich the nation-state found both its zenith and its nadir, its apotheosis and its Black Mass. Joining now the rank of the nation-states, Israel cannot but share in their decadence.

If anybody had been anxious to devise a textbook parody on the nation-state he could produce nothing better than the State of Israel with all its grotesque corridors, bulges, necks, and triangles, carved out by the master carvers of the United Nations.

Usually the irrationality of the nation-state is concentrated on its frontiers and customs walls, where nation is separated from nation. Inside a frontier, on tens or hundreds of thousands of square miles, millions of people have built their homes and more or less normal existences. Only beyond those spaces, at the next frontier, does the stark madness of the nation-state once again stare you in the face. In Israel you can never escape its mad stare: wherever you go you are always at some frontier or other:

'Look, on the hill over there are the *Syrians*!'

'The *Jordan* Arabs infiltrate this valley night after night!'

'Over there paces the *Egyptian* sentry.'

'Mind this path here—it takes you straight to the *Lebanon*, thirty yards from here!'

'We have built this power station underground—otherwise it would be destroyed on the first day of hostilities.'

'Here our railway runs three times into foreign territory.'

'Along this road we do not travel after dusk: it is too close to the frontier.'

In Jerusalem Moshe Sharett, the Prime Minister and Minister of Foreign Affairs, took me to the window of his office and showed me the sand dune outside and across it a belt of barbed wire. The Jordan-Israeli frontier, or demarcation line, ran within less than a stone's throw from here. The Minister of Foreign Affairs has only to lift his head from his desk to face the 'enemy'. If posterity ever erects a Museum of the Absurdities of the Nation-State, it should exhibit a picture showing this view from the Prime Minister's office. It should also exhibit the barbed wire that now cuts across the grounds of the French Hospital in Jerusalem; the sentry boxes on the Old Wall opposite Mount Zion; and the photographs of children shot dead while they were playing outside their homes amid barbed wire entanglements. The lunacy of the nation-state has come up to Jerusalem and cut in two the cradle of the world's religions.

By any normal standard Israel's economy is bankrupt. Her exports cover the cost of only a small fraction of the imports. Most of the deficit is paid out of the large pocket of American Jewry and by U.S. government aid. Israel buys expensive foods and raw materials for pounds and dollars and works hard to find remote markets for its own produce. In the old days the roads from Palestine to its Arab neighbours were crowded with lorries carrying food from the Arab countries to Israel and industrial goods towards them. Now trade is at a standstill because the Arab governments refuse to recognize Israel's political existence and persist in boycotting it.

The State of Israel has had explosives—the grievances of hundreds of thousands of displaced Arabs—built into its very foundations. One cannot in fairness blame the Jews for this. People pursued by a monster and running to save their lives cannot help injuring those who are in the way and cannot help trampling over their property. The Jews feel that the injury they have done to the Arabs is child's play compared with their own tragedy. This is true enough, but it does not prevent the Arabs from smarting under their grievance and craving revenge. To the Israelis Palestine is and never ceased to be Jewish. To the Arabs the Jews are and will for long remain invaders and intruders.

As long as a solution to the problem is sought in nationalist terms both Arab and Jew are condemned to move within a vicious circle of hatred and revenge. Arabs murder Jewish mothers and children. Jews stage the Kibiya massacre. The Arabs are only waiting for a turn in Middle East affairs which will allow them to crush Israel; in the meantime they watch intently for any false step Israel may make. Israel's hope is that the Arab states will for ever remain as backward, indolent, corrupt, and friendless as they were during the Arab-Jewish war; for otherwise the Israelis, even if their numbers were trebled, could not hold their ground against forty million Arabs. Each side sees its own security and prosperity in the insecurity, destitution, and distress of the other.

There seems to be no immediate way out of this predicament. In the long run a way out may be found beyond the nation-state, perhaps within the broader framework of a Middle East federation. Israel might then play among the Arab states a role as modest as are its numbers and as great as are its intellectual and spiritual resources. This idea, I am told, is beginning to gain ground among younger politicians and political thinkers on both sides; but it is not likely to gain much ground in the near future. The Jews are still too deeply intoxicated with their newly acquired nation-state and the Arabs are too fully obsessed with their grievance to look very far ahead. Any supra-national organization, like a Middle East federation, is sheer *Zukunftsmusik* to both. But sometimes it is only the music of the future to which it is worth listening.

# VI

# Israel's Tenth Birthday[1]

ISRAELIS 'from Dan to Beersheba' are about to celebrate the tenth anniversary of the creation of their State. They recollect with intense pride the heroism with which, in the spring of 1948, their men and women took up arms and wrested independence and statehood from the Arabs, the British, and the hesitant and intriguing diplomacies of the Great Powers. They also look back with satisfaction and confidence on the record of Israel's first decade, a record of great achievement in the building of a national life and culture.

The emergence of Israel is indeed, like all the long and dramatic history of the Jews, a phenomenon unique in its kind, a marvel and a prodigy of history, before which Jew and non-Jew alike stand in awe and amazement, wondering over its significance. This is the stuff of which in earlier epochs the great heroic myths and legends were created, such as the legends of Thermopylae and of the Maccabees.

It is therefore not surprising that Israelis should view their own experience with some exaltation. 'What is modern Israel,' says, for instance, Mr. Abba Eban, one of their eloquent statesmen, 'except the union of this people, land, and language in a sublime fulfilment of history's cycle, a

[1] *The Observer*, April 1958.

bridge thrown across the gulf of continents and generations, to symbolize the unity of all historic experience?' Yet one cannot help feeling that this solemnly romantic interpretation of the origins and meaning of Israel is unsatisfactory. It surrounds the facts, of which we have all been witnesses, with a golden mist of fiction. It throws a veil of fancy over the realities of the recent past; and it may conjure up dangerously unreal prospects before Israel.

We are no longer living in the age of heroic legend— such myths as our epoch has thrown up have all been shabby and extremely short-lived. Unique as the State of Israel stands in the modern world, it has not come into being as 'a sublime fulfilment of history's cycle ... to symbolize the unity of all historic experience.' It was not the Messianic yearning of the Jews for their Promised Land that gave birth to it. What are the facts?

Before the advent of Nazism, and even after it, the overwhelming majority of Jews refused to respond to the appeal of Zionism. Even in Eastern Europe, where they formed large and compact communities, spoke their own language, developed their own culture and literature, and suffered from savage discrimination, they considered themselves citizens of the countries in which they lived, and tied their future to the future of those countries, not to that of a Jewish Homeland in Palestine. A good half of Eastern European Jewry, especially its large and vigorous Labour movement, viewed the idea of such a Homeland with conscious and irreducible hostility. Zionism there was the nationalistic *mystique* of the Jewish middle class, which was not, however, willing to abandon its established positions and to uproot itself for the sake of its Zionist dream. Yet Eastern European Jewry formed the main reservoir from which Zionism drew its support—from there came most of its leaders, pioneers, and recruits. Elsewhere the response to Zionism was incomparably weaker.

Zionists may say—and who can deny it? that European Jewry would have survived if it had followed the call of Zionism. The fact is that the European Jews' hostility or lukewarmness towards the idea of a Jewish Homeland sprang from their trust in the nations among whom they lived, and from their deep confidence in the humanitarian traditions and prospects of European civilization. Zionism saw no future for the Jews in Europe—it was the political epitome of the Jewish distrust of the gentile world.

To Europe's eternal shame, that distrust has proved itself all too well justified. Only after this had become horribly clear, after six million out of the fifteen million European Jews had perished in gas chambers, and after Israelis had seen the British chase from the shores of Palestine ghost-like ships loaded with the wreckage of European Jewry, did the State of Israel become a reality. It came into being not as 'a sublime fulfilment of history's cycle' but as an act of Jewish despair—and a monument to the grimmest phase of European history, a phase of madness and decay.

In terms of practical policies, Israel has owed its existence and survival to a curious coincidence of circumstances which are hardly noticed when events are viewed from the height of a romantic nationalism. Israeli historians understandably dwell on the courage, ingenuity, and exploits of *Palmach*, the small Jewish Defence Corps which, although outnumbered and surrounded, inflicted defeat on several Arab armies. The Israelis were, however, favoured by certain factors.

The Arabs were utterly backward, divided against themselves, and friendless. Britain, her Empire dissolving, was retreating from the Middle East. The United States and the Soviet Union, the chief antagonists of the new era, were momentarily united against Britain and pressed her to retreat further. Outnumbered, the Jews enjoyed the advantages of superior European organization and training; and they drew the sinews of their war of independence and the weapons with which they fought from the United States and Eastern Europe. The outcome of the struggle might have been different if the Arabs had been less divided or better armed and better trained; if Britain had not been in retreat; and if either the Soviet Union or the United States had backed the Arabs.

This interplay of factors favourable to Israel was by its nature transitory. Of this, the leaders of Israel seem to be oblivious. Consciously or unconsciously they project the circumstances of 1948 into an indefinite future; and on this projection they base their policy. Although they are somewhat afraid of the backing that the Soviet rulers have recently given to Arab nationalism, the Israeli leaders seem confident that somehow they will always find more powerful friends in the world; and they assume that their Arab neighbours will for ever, or at any rate for a very long time, remain as backward and divided as they were ten years ago.

As if infected with the old European conceit and disdain for Asians and Africans (a disdain of which Europeans are slowly but surely curing themselves through bitter experience), the Israelis are evidently underrating the potentialities of their neighbours and their capacity for progress. Ben Gurion appears at times to be one of the last depositories of the philosophy of the white man's burden. No doubt the Suez adventure, and the poor account the Egyptians gave of themselves, have tended to confirm the Israelis in this conceit. If so, then the success of their arms in the Sinai Desert may well be worse, in its long-term consequences for Israel, than a defeat.

Here we come to the crux of Israel's relationship with the world: its attitude towards the rising nations of Asia and Africa. When one criticizes Israel's policy, one meets with the reply that the emergence of Israel should be seen as part of the awakening of the colonial and semi-colonial people. 'After all, this [criticism] applies to almost the whole of Asia and Africa,' says a progressive Zionist writer. 'Israel was not alone. There were India, Burma, Ceylon, Ghana, Nigeria, Morocco, Tunisia, Libya, the Sudan—and the process is continuing.'

Here again legend is confused with reality. The rise of India, Burma, and Ghana, etc., from colonial subjection to independent statehood has been an organic, social, and political process in a way in which the rise of Israel was not. What is worse, Israel has found itself in conflict open or latent, with so many of the rising nations of Asia and Africa. Israel cannot have it both ways: it cannot present itself as one of these nations and claim for itself the rights due to them and, at the same time, pursue its own interests, real or imaginary, in steady opposition to them or in haughty aloofness.

This opposition has been due partly to the circumstances in which the State of Israel was born—at its very birth it could not help trespassing upon the rights of the Arabs. But in its own interest Israel could and should have done everything in its power to assuage the Arab grievance and mitigate the antagonism. Instead, Israel has done nearly everything to exacerbate and perpetuate the antagonism— and through nothing so much as through the invasion of the Sinai. In the balance sheet of Israel's first decade this is a grave and dangerous liability which may in time out-weigh many impressive assets. In the long run, Israel cannot survive on the borders of Asia and Africa in conflict with Asia and Africa. It has become a haven of refuge for the survivors of European Jewry. Let it not become a death-trap for them!

It is a sad paradox of history that Jews should have acquired their own statehood only in the middle of this century, when from year to year the obsolescence of the nation-state is becoming more and more obvious. They were not associated with the nation-state in its heyday, when for so many people it was a factor of material and moral progress, when it marked an advance upon medieval particularisms, when it swept away the rubble of feudalism, and helped to free Europeans from spiritual bondage to the Church. Modern Jewry, in so far as its own mental horizons were not confined to synagogue and market place, gave Europe the greatest expounders of the universal view of man, from Spinoza to Marx.

The Jews were conditioned by the circumstances of their existence to rise above the limitations of the nationalist out-look, to overcome the fetishes of state or empire, and to look forward to supra-national forms of social existence. Now, however, when the nation-state is decaying, when it has become as crass an anachronism as the feudal prince-doms once were, and when the permanent revolution in technology makes the finding of supra-national forms of existence a matter of life or death for mankind, Jews are investing their boundless enthusiasm and their great talents in their own nation-state and their own nationalism.

This is not their fault; and the gentile world has no moral right to blame them. But the paradox is there; and Jews might as well grow more aware of it than they are. True, Israel cannot be expected to give the world the example and the lead in abandoning the nation-state for higher forms of social organization; but Israelis might at least take a more sober view of their predicament and chances, and beware of being carried away by their new-fangled and already red-hot nationalism. They also ought to get used to the idea that their state is not above criticism: it is an earthly creation not a Biblical sanctity, not a 'chosen' nation-state.

Once again we may be reminded of the nationalisms of the other 'young' nations, the Indians, the Egyptians, and so on. In the case of none of them, however, is the inconsistency so striking, because none of these peoples has a tradition of cosmopolitanism or internationalism comparable to the Jewish tradition. And, of course, the nationalism of those peoples is open to the same criticisms and objections.

The enthusiasm of a people striving to emancipate itself from foreign rule commands respect and admiration. But all too often it happens that after emancipation has been won, the enthusiasm continues to be boosted and is then abused and harnessed to policies which must command far less respect. For a subject people, independent statehood is a vital necessity and an advance; but once such a people has reached the stage of independence nothing can be more retrograde for it than to fix its mind on that stage and to refuse to look beyond it. The nationalism of a sovereign people cannot claim for itself the justification claimed by the nationalism of an oppressed people.

This is no matter of abstract principle only. The future of Israel may well depend on whether the Israelis are on guard against nationalist conceit and are able to find a common language with the peoples around them. Will they find it in the second decade of their statehood? There is nothing that a friend of the people of Israel can wish them more ardently.

# VII

# The Israeli-Arab War, June 1967[1]

THE war and the 'miracle' of Israel's victory have solved none of the problems that confront Israel and the Arab states. They have, on the contrary, aggravated all the old issues and created new, more dangerous ones. They have not increased Israel's security, but have rendered it more vulnerable than it had been before 5 June 1967. This 'six days wonder', this latest, all-too-easy triumph of Israeli arms will be seen one day, in a not very remote future, to have been a disaster in the first instance for Israel itself.

Let us consider the international background. We have to relate this war to the great power struggle and ideological conflicts in the world which form its context. In these last years American imperialism, and the forces associated with it and supported by it, have been engaged in a tremendous political, ideological, economic, and military offensive over a vast area of Asia and Africa; while the forces opposed to the American penetration, the Soviet Union in the first instance, have barely held their ground or have been in retreat. This trend emerges from a long series of events: the Ghanaian upheaval, in which Nkrumah's government was overthrown; the growth of reaction in various Afro-Asian countries; the bloody triumph of anti-Communism in

[1] From an interview given to the *New Left Review* on 23 June 1967.

Indonesia, which was a huge victory for counter-revolution in Asia; the escalation of the American war in Vietnam; and the 'marginal' right-wing military coup in Greece. The Arab-Israeli war was not an isolated affair; it belongs to this category of events. The counter-trend has manifested itself in revolutionary ferment in various parts of India, the radicalization of the political mood in Arab countries, the effective struggle of the National Front of Liberation in Vietnam; and the world-wide growth of opposition to American intervention. The advance of American imperialism and of Afro-Asian counter-revolution has not gone unopposed, but its success everywhere outside Vietnam has been evident.

In the Middle East the American forward push has been of relatively recent date. During the Suez war, the United States still adopted an 'anti-colonialist' stance. It acted, in seeming accord with the Soviet Union, to bring about the British and French withdrawal. The logic of American policy was still the same as in the late 1940s, when the State of Israel was in the making. As long as the American ruling class was interested primarily in squeezing out the old colonial Powers from Africa and Asia, the White House was a mainstay of 'anti-colonialism'. But having contributed to the débâcle of the old Empires, the United States took fright at the 'power vacuum' that might be filled by native revolutionary forces or the Soviet Union or a combination of both. Yankee anti-colonialism faded out, and America 'stepped in'. In the Middle East this happened during the period between the Suez crisis and the last Israeli war. The American military landings in Lebanon in 1958 were designed to stem a high tide of revolution in that area, especially in Iraq. Since then the United States, no doubt relying to some extent on Soviet 'moderation', has avoided open and direct military involvement in the Middle East and maintained a posture of detachment. This posture does not make the American presence there any less real.

\*      \*      \*

The Israelis have, of course, acted on their own motives, and not merely to suit the convenience of American policy. That their leaders and the great mass of Israelis believe themselves to be menaced by Arab hostility need not be doubted. That some 'bloodthirsty' Arab declarations about 'wiping Israel off the map' made Israeli flesh creep is evident. The Israelis are haunted by the memories of the Jewish tragedy in Europe and now feel isolated and encircled by the 'teeming' millions of a hostile Arab world. Nothing was easier for their own propagandists, aided by Arab verbal excesses, than to play up the fear of another 'final solution' threatening the Jews, this time in Asia. Conjuring up Biblical myths and all the ancient religious-national symbols of Jewish history, the propagandists whipped up that frenzy of belligerence, arrogance, and fanaticism of which the Israelis gave such startling displays as they rushed to Sinai and the Wailing Wall and to Jordan and the walls of Jericho. Behind the frenzy and arrogance there lay Israel's suppressed sense of guilt towards the Arabs, the feeling that the Arabs would never forget or forgive the blows Israel had inflicted on them: the seizure of their land, the fate of a million or more refugees, and repeated military defeats and humiliations. Driven half-mad by fear of Arab revenge, the Israelis have, in their overwhelming majority, accepted the 'doctrine' inspiring their government's policy, the 'doctrine' that holds that Israel's security lies in periodic warfare which every few years must reduce the Arab states to impotence.

Yet, whatever their own motives and fears, the Israelis are not and cannot be independent agents. The factors of Israel's dependence were to some extent 'built in' in its history over the last two decades. All Israeli governments have staked Israel's existence on the 'Western orientation'. This alone would have sufficed to turn Israel into a Western outpost in the Middle East, and so to involve it in the great conflict between imperialism (or neo-colonialism) and the Arab peoples struggling for their emancipation. Other factors have been in play as well. Israel's economy has depended for its tenuous balance and growth on foreign Zionist financial aid, especially on American donations. These donations have been a curse in disguise for the new state. They have enabled the government to manage its balance of payments in a way in which no country in the world can do it, without engaging in any trade with its neighbours. The influx of foreign funds has distorted Israel's economic structure by encouraging the growth of a large, unproductive sector and a standard of living which is not related to the country's own productivity and earnings.[1] This has, of course, unfailingly kept Israel well within the 'western sphere of influence'. Israel has in effect lived far above its means. Over many years nearly half of Israel's food was imported from the West. As the American administration exempts from taxation earnings and profits earmarked as donations for Israel, the Treasury in Washington has held its hand on the purses on which Israel's

[1] In recent years Israel has been receiving up to 250 million dollars annually in grants and loans from the western powers, in aid from the United States, and in contributions from Jews abroad. This amounts to nearly 125 dollars a year per head of the Israeli population.

economy depends. Washington could at any time hit Israel by refusing the tax exemption (even though this would lose it the Jewish vote in elections). The threat of such a sanction, never uttered but always present, and occasionally hinted at, has been enough to align Israeli policy firmly with the United States.

Years ago, when I visited Israel, a high Israeli official listed to me the factories that they could not build because of American objections—among them steel mills and plants producing agricultural machinery. On the other hand, there was a list of virtually useless factories turning out fantastic amounts of plastic kitchen utensils, toys, etc. Nor could any Israeli administration ever feel free to consider seriously Israel's vital, long-term need for trade and close economic ties with its Arab neighbours or for improving economic relations with the U.S.S.R. and Eastern Europe.

Economic dependence has affected Israel's domestic policy and 'cultural atmosphere' in other ways as well. The American donor is also the most important foreign investor operating in the Holy Land. A wealthy American Jew, a 'worldly businessman' among his gentile associates and friends in New York, Philadelphia or Detroit, is at heart proud to be a member of the Chosen People, and in Israel he exercises his influence in favour of religious obscurantism and reaction. A fervent believer in free enterprise, he views with a hostile eye even the mild 'socialism' of the Histradruth and the kibbutzim, and has done his bit in taming it. Above all, he has helped the rabbis to maintain their stranglehold on legislation and much of the education and so to keep alive the spirit of racial-talmudic exclusiveness and superiority. All this has fed and inflamed the antagonism towards the Arabs.

The cold war imparted great momentum to the reactionary trends in Israel and exacerbated the Arab-Jewish conflict. Israel was firmly committed to anti-communism. True, Stalin's policy in his last years, outbreaks of anti-semitism in the U.S.S.R., anti-Jewish *motifs* in the trials of Slansky, Rajk, and Kostov, and Soviet encouragement of even the most irrational forms of Arab nationalism, all bear their share of responsibility for Israel's attitude. Yet it should not be forgotten that Stalin had been Israel's godfather; that it was with Czechoslovak munitions, supplied on Stalin's orders, that the Jews had fought the British occupation army—and the Arabs—in 1947–48; and that the Soviet envoy was the first to vote for the recognition of the State of Israel by the United Nations. It may be argued that Stalin's change of attitude towards Israel was itself a reaction to Israel's alignment with the West. And in the post-Stalin era the Israeli governments have persisted in this alignment.

Irreconcilable hostility to Arab aspirations to unity and national emancipation from the West thus became *the* axiom of Israeli policy. Hence Israel's role in 1956, in the Suez war. Israel's Social Democratic ministers, no less than Western colonialists, have embraced a *raison d'état* which sees its highest wisdom in keeping the Arabs divided and backward and in playing their reactionary Hashemite and other feudal elements against the Republican, national-revolutionary forces. Early in 1967, when it seemed that a republican uprising or coup might overthrow King Hussein, Mr. Eshkol's government made no bones about it that, in case of a 'Nasserite coup' in Amman, Israeli troops would march into Jordan. And the prelude to the events of last June was provided by Israel's adoption of a menacing attitude towards Syria's new régime which it denounced as 'Nasserite' or even 'ultra-Nasserite' (for Syria's government appeared to be a shade more anti-imperialist and radical than Egypt's).

Did Israel, in fact, plan to attack Syria some time in May, as Soviet Intelligence Services believed and as Moscow warned Nasser? We do not know. It was as a result of this warning, and with Soviet encouragement, that Nasser ordered mobilization and concentration of troops on the Sinai frontier. If Israel had such a plan, Nasser's move may have delayed the attack on Syria by a few weeks. If Israel had no such plan, its behaviour gave to its anti-Syrian threats the kind of plausibility that Arab threats had in Israeli eyes. In any case, Israel's rulers were quite confident that their aggressiveness *vis-à-vis* either Syria or Egypt would meet with Western sympathy and bring them reward. This calculation underlay their decision to strike the pre-emptive blow on June 5th. They were absolutely sure of American, and to some extent British, moral, political, and economic support. They knew that no matter however far they went in attacking the Arabs, they could count on American diplomatic protection or, at the very least, on American official indulgence. And they were not mistaken. The White House and the Pentagon could not fail to appreciate men who for their own reasons, were determined to put down the Arab enemies of American neo-colonialism. General Dayan acted as a kind of Marshal Ky for the Middle East and appeared to be doing his job with startling speed, efficiency, and ruthlessness. He was, and is, a much cheaper and far less embarrassing ally than Ky.

\*    \*    \*

The Arab behaviour, especially Nasser's divided mind and hesitation on the eve of hostilities, presents a striking contrast to Israel's determination and uninhibited aggressiveness. Having, with Soviet encouragement, moved his troops to the Sinai frontier, and even put his Russian-made missiles in position, Nasser then, without consulting Moscow, proclaimed the blockade of the Straits of Tiran. This was a provocative move, though practically of very limited significance. The western powers did not consider it important enough to try and 'test' the blockade. It provided Nasser with a prestige gain and enabled him to claim that he had wrested from Israel the last fruit of their 1956 victory. (Before the Suez war Israeli ships could not pass these Straits.) The Israelis played up the blockade as a mortal danger to their economy, which it was not; and they replied by mobilizing their forces and moving them to the frontiers.

Soviet propaganda still continued to encourage the Arabs in public. However, a conference of Middle Eastern Communist Parties held in May (its resolutions were summarized in *Pravda*) was strangely reticent about the crisis and allusively critical of Nasser. More important were the curious diplomatic manoeuvres behind the scenes. On 26 May, in the dead of night (at 2.30 a.m.) the Soviet Ambassador woke up Nasser to give him a grave warning that the Egyptian army must not be the first to open fire. Nasser complied. The compliance was so thorough that he not only refrained from starting hostilities, but took no precautions whatsoever against the possibility of an Israeli attack: he left his airfields undefended and his planes grounded and uncamouflaged. He did not even bother to mine the Tiran Straits or to place a few guns on their shores (as the Israelis found to their surprise when they got there).

All this suggests hopeless bungling on Nasser's part and on the part of the Egyptian Command. But the real bunglers sat in the Kremlin. Brezhnev's and Kosygin's behaviour during these events was reminiscent of Khrushchev's during the Cuban crisis, though it was even more muddle-headed. The pattern was the same. In the first phase there was needless provocation of the other side and a reckless move towards the 'brink'; in the next sudden panic and a hasty retreat; and then followed frantic attempts to save face and cover up the traces. Having excited Arab fears, encouraged them to risky moves, promised to stand by them, and having brought out their own naval units into the Mediterranean to counter the moves of the American Sixth Fleet, the Russians then tied Nasser hand and foot.

Why did they do it? As the tension was mounting, the 'hot line' between the Kremlin and the White House went into action. The two super-powers agreed to avoid direct intervention and to curb the parties to the conflict. If the Americans went through the motions of curbing the Israelis, they must have done it so perfunctorily, or with so many winks that the Israelis felt, in fact, encouraged to go ahead with their plan for the pre-emptive blow. (We have, at any rate, not heard of the American Ambassador waking up the Israeli Prime Minister to warn him that the Israelis must not be the first to open fire.) The Soviet curb on Nasser was heavy, rude, and effective. Even so, Nasser's failure to take elementary military precautions remains something of a puzzle. Did the Soviet Ambassador in the course of his nocturnal visit tell Nasser that Moscow was sure that the Israelis would not strike first? Had Washington given

Moscow such an assurance? And was Moscow so gullible as to take it at face value and act on it? It seems almost incredible that this should have been so. But only some such version of the events can account for Nasser's inactivity and for Moscow's stunned surprise at the outbreak of hostilities.

Behind all this bungling there loomed the central contradiction of Soviet policy. On the one hand the Soviet leaders see in the preservation of the international *status quo*, including the social *status quo*, the essential condition of their national security and of 'peaceful co-existence'. They are therefore anxious to keep at a 'safe distance' from storm centres of class conflict in the world and to avoid dangerous foreign entanglements. On the other hand, they cannot, for ideological and power-political reasons, avoid altogether dangerous entanglements. They cannot quite keep at a safe distance when American neo-colonialism clashed directly or indirectly with its Afro-Asian and Latin-American enemies, who look to Moscow as their friend and protector. In normal times this contradiction is only latent, Moscow works for *détente* and rapprochement with the U.S.A.; and it cautiously aids and arms its Afro-Asian or Cuban friends. But sooner or later the moment of crisis comes and the contradiction explodes in Moscow's face. Soviet policy must then choose between its allies and protégés working against the *status quo*, and its own commitment to the *status quo*. When the choice is pressing and ineluctable, it opts for the *status quo*.

The dilemma is real and in the nuclear age dangerous enough. But it confronts the U.S.A. as well, for the U.S.A. is just as much interested as is the U.S.S.R. in avoiding world war and nuclear conflict. This, however, limits its freedom of action and of political-ideological offensive far less than it restricts Soviet freedom. Washington is far less afraid of the possibility that some move by one of its protégés, or its own military intervention, might lead to a direct confrontation of the super powers. After the Cuban crisis and the war in Vietnam, the Arab-Israeli war has once again sharply illuminated the difference.

*     *     *

To some extent the present situation has been determined by the whole course of Arab-Israeli relations since the second World War and even since the first. Yet I believe that some options were open to the Israelis. There is a parable with the help of which I once tried to present this problem to an Israeli audience.

A man once jumped from the top floor of a burning house in which many members of his family had already perished. He managed to save his life; but as he was falling he hit a person standing down below and broke that person's legs and arms. The jumping man had no choice; yet to the man with the broken limbs he was the cause of his misfortune. If both behaved rationally, they would not become enemies. The man who escaped from the blazing house, having recovered, would have tried to help and console the other sufferer; and the latter might have realized that he was the victim of circumstances over which neither of them had control. But look what happens when these people behave irrationally. The injured man blames the other for his misery and swears to make him pay for it. The other, afraid of the crippled man's revenge, insults him, kicks him, and beats him up whenever they meet. The kicked man again swears revenge and is again punched and punished. The bitter enmity, so fortuitous at first, hardens and comes to overshadow the whole existence of both men and to poison their minds.

You will, I am sure, recognize yourselves (I said to my Israeli audience), the remnants of European Jewry in Israel, in the man who jumped from the blazing house. The other character represents, of course, the Palestine Arabs, more than a million of them, who have lost their lands and their homes. They are resentful; they gaze from across the frontiers on their old native places; they raid you stealthily, and swear revenge. You punch and kick them mercilessly; you have shown that you know how to do it. But what is the sense of it? And what is the prospect?

The responsibility for the tragedy of European Jews, for Auschwitz, Majdanek, and the slaughters in the ghetto, rests entirely on our western bourgeois 'civilization', of which Nazism was the legitimate, even though degenerate, off-spring. Yet it was the Arabs who were made to pay the price for the crimes the West committed towards the Jews. They are still made to pay it, for the 'guilty conscience' of the West is, of course, pro-Israeli and anti-Arab. And how easily Israel had allowed itself to be bribed and fooled by the false 'conscience money'.

A rational relationship between Israelis and Arabs might have been possible if Israel had at least attempted to establish it, if the man who threw himself down from the burning house had tried to make friends with the innocent victim of his jump and to compensate him. This did not happen. Israel never even recognized the Arab grievance. From the outset Zionism worked towards the creation of a purely Jewish state and was glad to rid the country of its Arab inhabitants. No Israeli government has ever seriously looked for any opportunity to remove or assuage the grievance. They refused even to consider the fate of the huge mass of refugees unless the Arab states first recognized Israel, unless, that is, the Arabs surrendered politically before starting negotiations. Perhaps this might still be excused as bargaining tactics. The disastrous aggravation of Arab-Israeli relations was brought about by the Suez war, when Israel unashamedly acted as the spearhead of the old bankrupt European imperialisms in their last common stand in the Middle East, in their last attempt to maintain their grip on Egypt. The Israelis did not have to align them-selves with the shareholders of the Suez Canal Company. The pros and cons were clear; there was no question of any mixture of rights and wrongs on either side. The Israelis put themselves totally in the wrong, morally and politically.

On the face of it, the Arab-Israeli conflict is only a clash of two rival nationalisms, each moving within the vicious circle of its self-righteous and inflated ambitions. From the viewpoint of an abstract internationalism nothing would be easier than to dismiss both as equally worthless and reaction-ary. However, such a view would ignore the social and politi-cal realities of the situation. The nationalism of the people in semi-colonial or colonial countries, fighting for their independence, must not be put on the same moral-political level as the nationalism of conquerors and oppressors. The former has its historic justification and progressive aspect which the latter has not. Clearly, Arab nationalism, unlike the Israeli, still belongs to the former category.

Yet even the nationalism of the exploited and oppressed should not be viewed uncritically, for there are various phases in its development. In one phase progressive aspira-tions prevail; in another reactionary tendencies come to the surface. From the moment independence is won or nearly won, nationalism tends to shed its revolutionary aspect altogether and turns into a retrograde ideology. We have seen this happening in India, Indonesia, Israel, and to some extent even in China. And even in the revolutionary phase each nationalism has its streak of irrationality, an inclination to exclusiveness, national egoism and racism. Arab nationalism, despite all its historic merits and progressive functions, has also carried within itself these reactionary ingredients.

The June crisis has revealed some of the basic weaknesses of Arab political thought and action: the lack of political strategy; a proneness to emotional self-intoxication; and an excessive reliance on nationalist demagogy. These weaknesses were among the decisive causes of the Arab defeat. By indulging in threats of the destruction of Israel and even of 'extermination'—and how empty these threats were has been amply demonstrated by the Arabs' utter military unpreparedness—some of Egypt's and Jordan's propagandists provided plenty of grist to Israeli chauvinism, and enabled Israel's government to work up the mass of its people into the paroxysm of fear and ferocious aggressiveness which then burst upon Arab heads.

It is a truism that war is a continuation of policy. The six days' war has shown up the relative immaturity of the present Arab régimes. The Israelis owe their triumph not merely to the pre-emptive blow, but also to a more modern economic, political, and military organization. To some extent the war drew a balance on the decade of Arab development since the Suez war and has revealed its grave inadequacies. The modernization of the socio-economic structures of Egypt and the other Arab states and of Arab political thinking has proceeded far more slowly than people, inclined to idealize the present Arab régimes, have assumed.

The persisting backwardness is, of course, rooted in socio-economic conditions. But Arab ideology and methods of organization are in themselves factors of weakness. I have in mind the single party system, the cult of Nasserism, and the absence of free discussion. All this has greatly hampered the political education of the masses and the work of socialist enlightenment. The negative results have made themselves felt on various levels. When major decisions of policy depend on a more or less autocratic Leader, there is in normal times no genuine popular participation in the political processes, no vigilant and active consciousness, no initiative from below. This has had many consequences, even military ones. The Israeli pre-emptive blow, delivered with conventional weapons, would not have had such devastating impact if Egypt's armed forces had been accustomed to rely on the initiative of individual officers and soldiers. Local commanders would then have taken the elementary defensive precautions without waiting for orders from above. Military inefficiency reflected here a wider and deeper, social-political weakness. The military-bureaucratic methods of Nasserism also hamper the political integration of the Arab movement of liberation. Nationalist demagogy flourishes all too easily; but it is no substitute for a real impulse to national unity and for a real mobilization of popular forces against the divisive, feudal and reactionary elements. We have seen how, during the emergency, excessive reliance on a single Leader made the fate of the Arab states dependent in fact on Great Power intervention and accidents of diplomatic manoeuvre.

*    *    *

Paradoxically and grotesquely, the Israelis appear now in the role of the Prussians of the Middle East. They have now

won three wars against their Arab neighbours. Just so did
the Prussians a century ago defeat all their neighbours within a few years, the Danes, the Austrians, and the French.
The succession of victories bred in them an absolute confidence in their own efficiency, a blind reliance on the force
of their arms, chauvinistic arrogance, and contempt for other
peoples. I fear that a similar degeneration—for degeneration it is—may be taking place in the political character of
Israel. Yet as the Prussia of the Middle East, Israel can be
only a feeble parody of the original. The Prussians were at
least able to use their victories for uniting in their Reich all
German-speaking peoples living outside the Austro-
Hungarian Empire. Germany's neighbours were divided
among themselves by interest, history, religion, and language. Bismarck, Wilhelm II, and Hitler could play them off
against one another. The Israelis are surrounded by Arabs
only. Attempts to play off the Arab states against one another
are bound to fail in the end. The Arabs were at loggerheads
with one another in 1948, when Israel waged its first war; they
were far less divided in 1956, during Israel's second war; and
they formed a common front in 1967. They may prove far
more firmly united in any future confrontation with Israel.

The Germans have summed up their own experience in
the bitter phrase: '*Man kann sich totsiegen!*' 'You can drive
yourself victoriously into your grave.' This is what the Israelis have been doing. They have bitten off much more
than they can swallow. In the conquered territories and in
Israel there are now nearly a million and a half Arabs, well
over forty per cent of the total population. Will the Israelis
expel this mass of Arabs in order to hold 'securely' the
conquered lands? This would create a new refugee problem,
more dangerous and larger than the old one. Will they give

up the conquered territories? No, say most of their leaders. Ben Gurion, the evil spirit of Israeli chauvinism, urges the creation of an 'Arab Palestinian State' on the Jordan, that would be an Israeli Protectorate. Can Israel expect that the Arabs will accept such a Protectorate? That they will not fight it tooth and nail? None of the Israeli parties is prepared even to contemplate a bi-national Arab-Israeli state. Meanwhile great numbers of Arabs have been 'induced' to leave their homes on the Jordan, and the treatment of those who have stayed behind is far worse than that of the Arab minority in Israel that was kept under martial law for nineteen years. Yes, this victory is worse for Israel than a defeat. Far from giving Israel a higher degree of security, it has rendered it much more insecure. If Arab revenge and extermination is what the Israelis feared, they have behaved as if they were bent on turning a bogey into an actual menace.

*     *     *

There was a moment, at the cease-fire, when it looked as if Egypt's defeat had led to Nasser's downfall and to the undoing of the policy associated with his name. If that had happened, the Middle East would have almost certainly been brought back into the Western sphere of influence. Egypt might have become another Ghana or Indonesia. This did not happen, however. The Arab masses who came out in the streets and squares of Cairo, Damascus, and Beirut to demand that Nasser should stay in office, prevented it happening. This was one of those rare historic popular impulses that redress or upset a political balance within a few moments. This time, in the hour of defeat, the initiative from below worked with immediate impact. There are only very few cases in history when a people have stood by a defeated leader in this way. The situation is, of course, still fluid. Reactionary influences will go on working within the Arab states to achieve something like a Ghanaian or Indonesian coup. But for the time being neo-colonialism has been denied the fruit of Israel's 'victory'.

\* \* \*

'The Russians have let us down!' was the bitter cry that came from Cairo, Damascus, and Beirut in June. And when the Arabs saw the Soviet delegate at the United Nations voting, in unison with the Americans, for a cease-fire to which no condition for a withdrawal of the Israeli troops was attached, they felt utterly betrayed. 'The Soviet Union will now sink to the rank of a second- or fourth-rate power,' Nasser was reported to have told the Soviet Ambassador. The events appeared to justify the Chinese accusation of Soviet collusion with the United States. The débâcle aroused an alarm in Eastern Europe as well. 'If the Soviet Union could let Egypt down like this, may it not also let us down when we are once again confronted by German aggression?', the Poles and the Czechs wondered. The Yugoslavs, too, were outraged. Tito, Gomulka, and other leaders rushed to Moscow to demand an explanation and a rescue operation for the Arabs. This was all the more remarkable as the demand came from the 'moderates' and the 'revisionists' who normally stand for 'peaceful coexistence' and *rapprochement* with the U.S.A. It was they who now spoke of Soviet 'collusion with American imperialism'.

The Soviet leaders had to do something. The fact that the intervention of the Arab masses had saved the Nasser régime, unexpectedly provided Moscow with fresh scope for manoeuvre. After the great let down, the Soviet leaders again came to the fore as the friends and protectors of the Arab states. A few spectacular gestures, breaking off diplomatic relations with Israel, and speeches at the United Nations, cost them little. Even the White House showed 'understanding' for Moscow's 'predicament' and for the 'tactical necessity' which presently brought Kosygin to the United Nations Assembly.

However, something more than gestures was required to restore the Soviet position. The Arabs demanded that the Soviet Union should at once help them to re-build their military strength, the strength they had lost through compliance with Soviet advice. They asked for new planes, new tanks, new guns, new stocks of munitions. But apart from the cost this involved—the value of the military equipment lost by Egypt alone is put at a billion pounds—the reconstitution of the Arab armed forces carries, from Moscow's viewpoint, major political risks. The Arabs refuse to negotiate with Israel; they may well afford to leave Israel to choke on its victory. Rearmament is Cairo's top priority. Israel has taught the Egyptians a lesson: next time the Egyptian air force may strike the pre-emptive blow. And Moscow has had to decide whether it will supply the weapons for that blow.

Moscow cannot favour the idea of such an Arab retaliation, but neither can it refuse to rearm Egypt. Yet Arab rearmament will almost certainly tempt Israel to interrupt the process and strike another pre-emptive blow in which case the Soviet Union would once again be faced with the dilemma which has worsted it in May and June. If Egypt were to strike first, the United States would almost certainly intervene. Its Sixth Fleet would not look on from the Mediterranean if the Israeli air force were knocked out and the Arabs were about to march into Jerusalem or Tel Aviv. If the U.S.S.R. again kept out of the conflict, it would irretrievably destroy its international power position.

A week after the cease-fire the Soviet Chief of Staff was in Cairo; and Soviet advisers and experts crowded the hotels there, beginning to work on the reconstitution of Egypt's armed forces. Yet Moscow cannot face with equanimity the prospect of an Arab-Israeli competition in pre-emptive blows and its wider implications. Probably the Soviet experts in Cairo were making haste slowly, while Soviet diplomacy tried to 'win the peace' for the Arabs after it had lost them the war. But even the most clever playing for time cannot solve the central issue of Soviet policy. How much longer can the Soviet Union adapt itself to the American forward push? How far can it retreat before the American economic-political and military offensives across the Afro-Asian area? Not for nothing did *Krasnaya Zvezda* already in June suggest that the current Soviet conception of peaceful coexistence might be in need of some revision. The military, and not they alone, fear that Soviet retreats are increasing the dynamic of the American forward push; and that if this goes on a direct Soviet-American clash may become inevitable. If Brezhnev and Kosygin do not manage to cope with this issue, changes in leadership are quite possible. The Cuban and Vietnamese crises contributed to Khrushchev's downfall. The full consequences of the Middle Eastern crisis have yet to unfold.

\*     \*     \*

I do not believe that the conflict between Arabs and Israelis can be resolved by military means. To be sure, no one can deny the Arab states the right to reconstitute their armed forces to some extent. But what they need far more urgently is a social and political strategy and new methods in their struggle for emancipation. This cannot be a purely negative strategy dominated by the anti-Israeli obsession. They may refuse to parley with Israel as long as Israel has not given up its conquests. They will necessarily resist the occupation régime on the Jordan and in the Gaza strip. But this need not mean a renewal of war.

The strategy that can yield the Arabs far greater gain than those that can be obtained in any Holy War or through a pre-emptive blow, a strategy that would bring them real victory, a civilized victory, must be centred on the imperative and urgent need for an intensive modernization of the structure of the Arab economy and of Arab politics and on the need for a genuine integration of Arab national life, which is still broken up by the old, inherited and imperialist-sponsored frontiers and divisions. These aims can be promoted only if the revolutionary and socialist tendencies in Arab politics are strengthened and developed.

Finally, Arab nationalism will be incomparably more effective as a liberating force if it is disciplined and rationalized by an element of internationalism that will enable the Arabs to approach the problem of Israel more realistically than hitherto. They cannot go on denying Israel's right to exist and indulging in bloodthirsty rhetoric. Economic growth, industrialization, education, more efficient organization and more sober policies are bound to give the Arabs what sheer numbers and anti-Israeli fury have not been able to give them, namely an actual preponderance which should almost automatically reduce Israel to its modest proportions and its proper role in the Middle East.

This is not, of course, a short term programme. Yet its realization need not take too much time; and there is no shorter way to emancipation. The short cuts of demagogy, revenge, and war have proved disastrous enough. Meanwhile, Arab policy should be based on a direct appeal to the Israeli people over the heads of the Israeli government, on an appeal to the workers and the kibbutzim. The latter should be freed from their fears by clear assurances and pledges that Israel's legitimate interests are respected and that Israel may even be welcome as a member of a future Middle Eastern Federation. This would cause the orgy of Israeli chauvinism to subside and would stimulate opposition to Eshkol's and Dayan's policy of conquest and domination. The capacity of Israeli workers to respond to such an appeal should not be underrated.

More independence from the Great Power game is also necessary. That game has distorted the social-political development of the Middle East. I have shown how much American influence has done to give Israel's policy its present repulsive and reactionary character. But Russian influence has also done something to warp Arab minds by feeding them with arid slogans, by encouraging demagogy, while Moscow's egoism and opportunism have fostered disillusionment and cynicism. If Middle East policy continues to be merely a plaything of the Great Powers, the prospect will be bleak indeed. Neither Jews nor Arabs will be able to break out of their vicious spirals. This is what we, of the Left, should be telling both the Arabs and the Jews as clearly and bluntly as we can.

\*     \*     \*

The confusion of the international Left has been undeniable and widespread. I shall not speak here of such 'friends of Israel' as M. Mollet and his company, who, like

Lord Avon and Selwyn Lloyd, saw in this war a continuation of the Suez campaign and their revenge for their discomfiture in 1956. Nor shall I waste words on the right-wing Zionist lobby in the Labour Party. But even on the 'extreme Left' of that party men like Sidney Silverman behaved in a way that might have been designed to illustrate someone's saying: 'Scratch a Jewish left-winger and you find only a Zionist.'

But the confusion showed itself even further on the Left and affected people with an otherwise unimpeachable record of struggle against imperialism. A French writer known for his courageous stand against the wars in Algeria and Vietnam this time called for solidarity with Israel, declaring that, if Israel's survival demanded American intervention, he would favour it and even raise the cry '*Vive le Président Johnson*'. Didn't it occur to him how incongruous it was to cry '*A bas Johnson!*' in Vietnam and '*Vive!*' in Israel? Jean-Paul Sartre also called, though with reservations, for solidarity with Israel, but then spoke frankly of the confusion in his own mind and its reasons. During the second World War, he said, as a member of the Resistance he learned to look upon the Jew as upon a brother to be defended in all circumstances. During the Algerian war the Arabs were his brothers, and he stood by them. The present conflict was therefore for him a fratricidal struggle in which he was unable to exercise cool judgment and was overwhelmed by conflicting emotions.

Still, we must exercise our judgment and must not allow it to be clouded by emotions and memories, however deep or haunting. We should not allow even invocations of Auschwitz to blackmail us into supporting the wrong cause. I am speaking as a Marxist of Jewish origin, whose next-of-kin perished in Auschwitz and whose relatives live in Israel. To justify or condone Israel's wars against the Arabs is to render Israel a very bad service indeed and to harm its own long-term interest. Israel's security, let me repeat, was not enhanced by the wars of 1956 and 1967; it was undermined and compromised by them. The 'friends of Israel' have in fact abetted Israel in a ruinous course.

They have also, willy-nilly, abetted the reactionary mood that took hold of Israel during the crisis. It was only with disgust that I could watch on television the scenes from Israel in those days; the displays of the conquerors' pride and brutality; the outbursts of chauvinism; and the wild celebrations of the inglorious triumph, all contrasting sharply with the pictures of Arab suffering and desolation, the treks of Jordanian refugees and the bodies of Egyptian soldiers killed by thirst in the desert. I looked at the medieval figures of the rabbis and *khassidim* jumping with joy at the Wailing Wall; and I felt how the ghosts of Talmudic obscurantism—and I know these only too well—crowded in on the country, and how the reactionary atmosphere in Israel had grown dense and stifling. Then came the many interviews with General Dayan, the hero and saviour, with the political mind of a regimental sergeant-major, ranting about annexations and venting a raucous callousness about the fate of the Arabs in the conquered areas. ('What do they matter to me?' 'As far as I am concerned, they may stay or they may go.') Already wrapped in a phoney military legend—the legend is phoney for Dayan neither planned nor conducted the six days' campaign—he cut a rather sinister figure, suggesting a candidate for the dictator's post: the hint was conveyed that if the civilian parties get too 'soft' on the Arabs this new Joshua, this mini-de Gaulle, will teach them a lesson, himself take power, and raise Israel's 'glory' even higher. And behind Dayan there was Beigin, Minister and leader of the extreme right-wing Zionists, who had long claimed even Trans-Jordania as part of 'historic' Israel. A reactionary war inevitably breeds the heroes, the moods, and the consequences in which its character and aims are faithfully mirrored.

On a deeper historical level the Jewish tragedy finds in Israel a dismal sequel. Israel's leaders exploit in self-justification, and over-exploit Auschwitz and Treblinka; but their actions mock the real meaning of the Jewish tragedy.

European Jews paid a horrible price for the role they had played in past ages, and not of their own choosing, as representatives of a market economy, of 'money', among peoples living in a natural, money-less, agricultural economy. They were the conspicuous carriers of early capitalism, traders and money lenders, in pre-capitalist society. The image of the rich Jewish merchant and usurer lived on in gentile folklore and remained engraved on the popular mind, stirring distrust and fear. The Nazis seized this image, magnified it to colossal dimensions, and constantly held it before the eyes of the masses.

August Bebel once said that anti-semitism is the 'socialism of the fools'. There was plenty of that kind of 'socialism' about, and all too little of the genuine socialism, in the era of the Great Slump, and of the mass unemployment and mass despair of the 1930s. The European working classes were unable to overthrow the bourgeois order; but the hatred of capitalism was intense and widespread enough to force an outlet for itself and focus on a scapegoat. Among the lower middle classes, the *lumpenbourgeoisie* and the *lumpenproletariat*, a frustrated anti-capitalism merged with fear of communism and neurotic xenophobia. The impact of Nazi Jew-baiting was so powerful in part because the image of the Jew as the alien and vicious 'blood-sucker' was to all too many people still an actuality. This accounted also for the relative indifference and the passivity with which so many non-Germans viewed the slaughter of the Jews. The socialism of the fools gleefully watched Shylock led to the gas chamber.

Israel promised not merely to give the survivors of the European-Jewish communities a 'National Home' but also to free them from the fatal stigma. This was the message of the kibbutzim, the Histadruth, and even of Zionism at large. The Jews were to cease to be unproductive elements, shopkeepers, economic and cultural interlopers, carriers of capitalism. They were to settle in 'their own land' as 'productive workers'.

Yet they now appear in the Middle East once again in the invidious role of agents not so much of their own, relatively feeble, capitalism, but of powerful western vested interests and as *protégés* of neo-colonialism. This is how the Arab world sees them, not without reason. Once again they arouse bitter emotions and hatreds in their neighbours, in all those who have ever been or still are victims of imperialism. What a fate it is for the Jewish people to be made to appear in this role! As agents of early capitalism they were still pioneers of progress in feudal society; as agents of the late, over-ripe, imperialist capitalism of our days, their role is altogether lamentable; and they are placed once again in the position of potential scapegoats. Is Jewish history to come full circle in such a way? This may well be the outcome of Israel's 'victories'; and of this Israel's real friends must warn it.

The Arabs, on the other hand, need to be put on guard against the socialism or the anti-imperialism of the fools. We trust that they will not succumb to it; and that they will learn from their defeat and recover to lay the foundations of a truly progressive, a socialist Middle East.

# VIII

# Marc Chagall
## and the Jewish Imagination[1]

FRANZ Meyer's *Marc Chagall* is, I am sure, the most
comprehensive study of the artist. I have read the six
hundred pages of its text with unflagging attention and have
spent many hours contemplating its beautiful reproductions.
The book is as informative on the latest phases of Chagall's
art as it is on the earliest; and what the author says about
Chagall's early paintings, and what the artist himself says
about them in *My Life*, brought back to me memories of my
own adolescent fascination with Chagall in the early 1920s.

Meyer is Chagall's son-in-law; and this monograph is
clearly a work of filial love and piety as well as of insight and
analysis.

Meyer reflects, as he puts it, on the 'significance of
Chagall's painting' and 'its place in contemporary art'.
Chagall, he says, 'stands in opposition to much that charac-
terizes our time: to the rationality of science, to utilitarian-
ism, and to the anonymous effect of technical progress'.
The painter considers it his 'mission' to struggle against the
'disease of rationalization' and to make us aware of 'the in-
ward reality of our souls'. Perhaps it is unfair to make on an

[1] B.B.C. Third Programme, 12 August 1965.

artist's behalf a claim to so absolute and edifying a philosophy, or to take such a claim literally if the artist himself makes it.

Another critic, quoted by Meyer, comes perhaps closer to the truth of the matter when, contrasting Chagall with Picasso, he points out that while Picasso represents the supreme triumph of the analytical intellect in art, Chagall's painting is the apotheosis of feeling and emotion. Objectivity is Picasso's artistic ideal, subjectivity—Chagall's. This is what Meyer too is trying to say, but he obscures it through overstatement.

Already in his youthful works, those painted before 1910, Chagall was the forerunner of Surrealism; German art historians describe him as the originator of Expressionism. With Chagall, says André Breton, dream and metaphor conquered modern painting.

From the outset the motifs of his dream-like vision are fixed; the same fragments of outward reality occur again and again in the stream of his fantasy; and it is a single stream of fantasy that runs through all his pictures—a single dream dreamt and painted in an immense multitude of variations.

Throughout his study Meyer stresses the religious-Jewish background of Chagall (although in his conclusion he says that this was only one of the elements determining Chagall's outlook). He maintains that 'the waters of Jewish mysticism had always nourished the roots of his forebears' spiritual world and thus the sources of his art', and that Chagall's 'fundamental anti-realism accords with the iconoclasm of Judaism'.

Again and again Meyer refers to Khassidism, the religious romanticism of Eastern European Jewry, and even to the medieval Cabbala, as the sources of the painter's inspiration.

Chagall's Jewishness is undeniable—he is steeped in

Jewish folklore. But his alleged indebtedness to the Cabbala and to the Jewish theological heritage is hardly credible. Least of all can it be said that his Surrealism accords in any way with rabbinical Jewry. Judaism's hostility towards the visual arts is notorious. By enforcing rigorously the commands, 'Thou shalt not make any graven image', rabbinical orthodoxy stunted the growth of the visual arts far more cruelly than even Calvinism did.

The walls of the Synagogue were bare and grim, even though sublime liturgical poetry and song resounded under its roof. The little town within the Jewish pale of Eastern Europe, the *Shtetl*, had its superb cantors and musicians, its bards, poets, and composers of folk tales; but it had no painters or sculptors. Even the Khassidic revolt against Talmudic scholasticism did not weaken the millennia-old abhorrence of the 'graven image'; and the Khassidic revivalism too quickly ossified into yet another rabbinical orthodoxy.

It was in defiance of tradition, outside the Synagogue, in opposition to it, that the Russian or Polish Jew began to paint; and it was only just before the close of the nineteenth century that he did so. Isaak Ilyich Levitan, the master of the Russian landscape, made his career in the 1880s and 1890s; but he grew up outside the pale.

Within the pale, the first generation of Jewish painters came to the fore later—and Chagall may still be counted as one of that generation, one of the pioneers. For a Jew to paint was to rise in revolt, to achieve an act of emancipation. The revolt was directed against Jewish clerical obscurantism as well as against Russian oppression. Around 1905, the Red Flag cast its reflection on the painter's canvas. Chagall took to the palette just after the defeat of the 1905 revolution, when a mood of despondency and resignation was spreading within the Jewish pale and without. The Jewish intelligentsia repented of their revolutionary 'follies'; and, with J. L. Peretz, their leader, were on the 'way back to the Synagogue'. Yet in Chagall, and through him, the long suppressed visual imagination of the Jew burst out like a volcano exploding in rainbows.

Yet, for all its implicit rebellion against the constricting tradition of Judaism, Chagall's painting is Jewish in a sense in which the cosmopolitan painting of Modigliani or Soutine is not. In most of his work, which is uncompromisingly representational and symbolist, he is the painter of his native *Shtetl* Vitebsk. On it his vision is focused. He paints its crooked, narrow streets and houses while he is there on the spot; he goes on painting them later in Paris, where he sets them under the arches of the Eiffel Tower; and he sees them again in bloodsoaked nightmares during the holocaust of Eastern European Jewry. He paints the *Shtetl* of the hewers of wood and drawers of water, not that of the middle classes.

His father, familiar to us from so many paintings, spent his life in the back-breaking labour of a porter, pushing barrels of herring for local traders. The multi-coloured apparitions which people Chagall's surrealistic world are beggars and butchers, cattle-dealers and soldiers, petty shop-keepers, itinerant preachers, and homeless fiddlers. Sometimes he draws Jews, who in their majestic dignity look like descendants of Rembrandt's rabbis. But as he himself tells us, these were beggars whom he would dress in his father's prayer shawl and phylacteries before he made them sit for him.

Even the interiors he paints, the *isbas*, the rickety and poverty-laden bedsteads, tables, chairs, and cloaks, so realistic in their dream-like unreality, belong recognizably to his parental home; he gives soul to the poverty of the *Shtetl* and turns it into poetry. And when he portrays Bella, his fiancée and wife, the daughter of a wealthy Jewish family of Vitebsk, he views her from a distance, looks up to her, and underlines her social status, as if he were painting a Spanish princess.

Looking back on Chagall's early works one is struck by the precocious revelation of his artistic personality. The untutored beginner of the years between 1907 and 1910 was already, with breath-taking originality and courage, giving shape to his vision in *The Musicians, The Wedding, The Couple, The Holy Family, Circumcision*, and *La Kermesse*. Almost at once Chagall found his expression, his feeling for nature, his mood, and his life-long motifs.

Early enough he absorbed the influence of Cézanne, Van Gogh, and Gauguin; but these influences, having enriched him, dissolved, as it were, within his artistic constitution. Of his first reactions to the avant-garde of Paris, Meyer says: 'Chagall borrowed from the Cubists . . . a few formal devices . . . the geometrical division of space . . . the cubistically articulated division of the figures.' But, he goes on, 'Cubism never exerted a truly formative influence on him, and his cubisation of the picture plane and the figures is always a superficial phenomenon. . . .'

If Chagall's response to Picasso and Cubism was ambivalent, his reaction to the early Russian expounders of abstract art, especially to Malevich and the so-called Suprematists, was one of outright hostility. Non-representational painting is to him a contradiction in terms; and his vision of the world is hermetic and intolerant of alien intrusions.

The spontaneity of Chagall's surrealism testifies, of course, to the universality of artistic ideas. This new 'ism' must

have been in the air if, in his Vitebsk backwater, he antici-
pated it even before the intelligentsia of the Russian capital
cities had an inkling of this new 'Freudian' approach to art.

Perhaps only a young painter, quite unencumbered by
academic routine, could so boldly disregard the realistic
and naturalistic conventionalities that still dominated
Russian painting. But Chagall's surrealism sprang also from
his Jewish imagination. It may be said that the entire existence
of the Russian Jews within the pale was 'surrealistic'.

Ground down by poverty and persecution, shaken by
pogroms, numbed by an archaic Messianic faith, torn between hopes held out by Zionism on the one hand, and
revolutionary socialism on the other, Eastern European Jewry
was hovering over the precipice. The Jewish *Luftmensch*,
economically unproductive and rootless, struggled helplessly
yet tenaciously for survival, and survived as if by miracle.

In his fantasy he raised himself above the realities of his
existence and scaled dizzy heights of wish-fulfilment only to
be hurled down again and again in rude awakenings. The
Jewish imagination sought to escape reality or to make life
fluid, bright, unpredictably miraculous; and Jewish humour
and self-irony cried and laughed over the constant clash
between hopes and realities.

Sholem Aleikhem created in his Menakhem Mendel the
Jewish Quixote of Eastern Europe, a figure as sublime and
grotesque as the old Knight Errant, but one which also in-
cluded Sancho Panza within his character. This Jewish mood
was the source of Chagall's feeling. In his imagination, too,
dream and reality are not polarized, not separated from one
another.

He looks at the world with the hazy and feverish eye of
the Jewish child, the *kheder* boy, for whom the age of

miracles is still alive. And so lovers *do* float over the roofs of Vitebsk; a beggar *is* or may be a fallen angel, if not some other magic power, or a charmed animal; and the stars *do* respond to the melody the bearded fiddler plays to them from a roof-top. Therein lies the secret of Chagall's art: in it, the native imagination of the Jewish child wrestles with the nightmares of the Jewish existence.

Chagall, however, is not the Jew at large; he is the Russian Jew. He often writes his nostalgia into the fringes of his pictures; and he does it in the Russian as well as in the Yiddish-Hebrew alphabet. The *muzhik's* world constantly impinges on the Jewish Vitebsk; and Chagall paints *I and the Village* in variant after variant.

Although some of his Jews look like the descendants of those rabbis and merchants of seventeenth-century Amsterdam whom Rembrandt had portrayed, most of them, including Chagall's own parents, resemble their Byelorussian and Greek Orthodox peasant-neighbours.

Indeed, there is in Chagall much of the Russian peasant poet. There is a close affinity between his surrealism and Sergei Yessenin's 'Imaginism'. Like Yessenin, Chagall reminds you of the *muzhik* of the folktale who has managed to 'catch the sun and light up his *isba* with it'. To both metaphor is essential.

Chagall too 'bows to the image of the cow over the butcher's shop' and is ready 'to carry the tail of a Russian horse like the train of a bridal gown'. Both also reacted to the Russian revolution in a similar manner: both responded to its early heroic appeal, and both were affected by subsequent disillusionment and moral depression.

In Chagall's *War on Palaces* a giant of a peasant carries a landlord's mansion on his head and stumps the earth. The revolution suddenly opened undreamt-of horizons before Chagall.

He was appointed Commissar of Art for the Vitebsk Province; backed by Lunacharsky, Lenin's great Commissar of Education, he opened his Academy of Art into which the children of illiterate Byelorussian *muzhiks* and Jewish toilers flocked *en masse*. This was an unprecedented and thrilling experience: art, daring *avant garde* art, was being carried to the people.

Then, when the Yiddish State Theatre was opened in Moscow, Chagall began his great work for that theatre and produced his murals and stage designs for the plays of Gogol, Chekhov, and Sholem Aleikhem. To grasp the extraordinary impact of the opening in Moscow of the Yiddish State Theatre, one has to remember that under the Tsars, Moscow, the Holy of Holies of Greek Orthodoxy, was practically out of bounds for Jews. Chagall had the ambition to 'turn the Yiddish Theatre into a world theatre'; and the style of his stage-designing did indeed leave its mark on all advanced Russian stage-craft of those years.

This was a great and inspiring time; but already in the early twenties the anti-climax was there: Chagall found himself hemmed in between the hostile doctrinaires of abstract art and the party officialdom which was already crying out for the utility art of 'socialist realism'. Discouraged, he left Moscow and Russia in 1922.

Behind Chagall's artistic predicament lay a tragedy more fundamental. The revolution had liberated the *Shtetl* from Tsarist oppression but had also doomed its way of life, its religious tradition, its small traders and artisans, and its *Luftmenschen*.

Here again there is an analogy between Chagall and Yessenin, for the revolution had likewise emancipated

Yessenin's *muzhiks* and doomed their archaic way of life. 'I am the countryside's last poet', said Yessenin. 'Like a wooden clock, the moon will grind out my last hour'. Chagall was to be the last painter of the *Shtetl*: the wooden clock and the moon grinding out 'the last hour' are there on so many of his canvases.

Yet even in Berlin, Paris, and New York, Chagall went on living on memories of his Vitebsk and his Russia—but now he sought refuge in the Jewish tradition, immersing himself in it deeper and deeper.

The Jew, clasping the sacred Scrolls in his arms and rescuing them from flames, becomes a constant motif in Chagall's pictures: so does the Wandering Jew, who amid all the world's upheavals goes his preordained way. We see both these motifs at the centre and in the foreground of *The Revolution*, which Chagall painted in 1937.

By the side of a praying Jew we see a Lenin-like figure, turned upside down, and Red Flags and scenes of the Russian civil war in the crowded background. This was an ambitious yet confused composition: it lacked focus in form as well as idea; it testified to Chagall's bafflement by his theme; and he himself cut up the picture into pieces.

Yet Chagall is not by temperament a tragic artist; he has had tragedy thrust upon him. The decade after his return to Western Europe, the period between 1923 and 1933, was for him a time of respite, enjoyment, and triumph. He never had in him anything of the restlessness which perpetually drives Picasso to negate and repudiate himself and his own achievement.

Chagall is inclined to self-contented serenity, even to complacency. He is 'optimistic'; he seeks reassurance and consolation in the 'biological permanence of life'. Yet the ordeal of European Jewry comes to fill his canvases. He paints his *Guernica* or rather his Guernicas, the long series of his *Crucifixions*, Crucifixions in red, in white, in blue, in yellow. Chagall's Christ, as Meyer points out, is not Christian; he is the epitome of the Jewish martyrdom. He is 'stretched in all his immense pain above the world of horrors. [Around him] men are hunted, persecuted, murdered'.

Always wrapped in the Jewish prayer shawl, he sometimes wears the cloth cap and the ragged trousers of a poor Vitebsk Jew; below him, on the earth, are crowds of terror-stricken and fleeing Jews; synagogues and sacred Scrolls are going up in fire and smoke. And while in Christian representations all suffering is concentrated in Christ and is overcome by His sacrifices, in Chagall's Crucifixions Christ does not vanquish suffering.

'Chagall's Christ figure', Meyer writes, 'lacks the Christian concept of salvation. For all his holiness he is by no means divine. [He] is a *man* who suffers pain in a thousand forms . . . [who] is eternally burned by the fire of the world and yet . . . remains indestructible.'

Finally, we see not one but many Christ figures, in the work-a-day clothes of poor Jews, stretched on crosses along the familiar narrow and crooked streets of Chagall's Vitebsk. And Chagall takes Christ back into Jewish history; in the *Crossing of the Red Sea*, painted in the years 1954 and 1955, he opens a symbolic perspective on the destiny of the Jews with the towering figure of Moses in the forefront and the Jewish Martyr on the Cross in the distant background. Chagall's vision grows in power, sharpness, and intensity. Yet underlying it all is his reconciliation with Jewish history, his surrender to it. He denounces and condemns no one. Over the ashes of Majdanek and Auschwitz he weeps his *Kaddish*, the great prayer for the dead.

# IX

# The Jewish Tragedy and the Historian

To a historian trying to comprehend the Jewish holocaust the greatest obstacle will be the absolute uniqueness of the catastrophe. This will be not just a matter of time and historical perspective. I doubt whether even in a thousand years people will understand Hitler, Auschwitz, Majdanek, and Treblinka better than we do now. Will they have a better historical perspective? On the contrary, posterity may understand it all even less than we do.

Did the Jews and the gentiles of the Age of Enlightenment and rationalism understand the Spanish Inquisition better than did the Jews who lived under the rule of Ferdinand and Isabella? And the *auto-da-fés* of the Inquisition were child's play compared with Auschwitz and Majdanek. There was still some human logic in the Inquisition, which treated the Jews as it treated other infidels and heretics, allowed them to survive physically, and even rewarded them if they were prepared to surrender spiritually.

The fury of Nazism, which was bent on the unconditional extermination of every Jewish man, woman, and child within its reach, passes the comprehension of a historian, who tries to uncover the motives of human behaviour and to discern the interests behind the motives. Who can analyse the motives and the interests behind the enormities of Auschwitz?

I am sure that it is not my personal involvement in the Jewish catastrophe that would prevent me, even now, as a historian, from writing objectively about it. It is rather the fact that we are confronted here by a huge and ominous mystery of the degeneration of the human character that will forever baffle and terrify mankind.

Perhaps a modern Aeschylus and Sophocles could cope with this theme: but they would do so on a level different from that of historical interpretation and explanation.

Printed in the United States
by Baker & Taylor Publisher Services